My Life as a Car

A Mental Wellness Guide
in Your Glove Compartment

My Life as a Car

A Mental Wellness Guide
in Your Glove Compartment

Elaine A. Campbell M.D.

**PSYCHE
BOOKS**

Winchester, UK
Washington, USA

First published by Psyche Books, 2012
Psyche Books is an imprint of John Hunt Publishing Ltd., Laurel House, Station Approach,
Alresford, Hants, SO24 9JH, UK
office1@jhpbooks.net
www.johnhuntpublishing.com
www.psyche-books.com

For distributor details and how to order please visit the 'Ordering' section on our website.

A CIP catalogue record for this book is available from the British Library.

Design: Lee Nash

Printed in the USA by Edwards Brothers Malloy

We operate a distinctive and ethical publishing philosophy in all
areas of our business, from our global network of authors to
production and worldwide distribution.

CONTENTS

To my husband, Dr. Jim Psarras, who makes all of my impromptu
car trips possible;
to my son Peter, whose brilliance and talents serve as
my driving force;
to my beautiful daughter, Molly,
whose devotion and love for mankind makes car trips a pure joy;
and to my beloved son, Andy.
Your smile will guide my way tonight.
I'll see you in my dreams.

Preface

The title was born the day I was at my auto mechanics. The car was not running well, and one of those yellow warning lights came on a mile or two down the road. I don't know which one, just that I was scolded once when I let it turn red, and my wallet also took a beating. Anyway, he just plugs some contraption into the electrical system and not only prints out a solution to the problem but also alerts me to other possible problems that may result in future mishaps.

Well, isn't that special? We have a detector that can pinpoint problems in our car.

And yes, when I go to my physician for my yearly, or thereabouts, checkup, I too am poked and prodded, and the results of my blood work and a good physical exam can also detect problems or rule them out. She checked me out just like my mechanic did – my car, not me.

I also noted that my glove compartment has maintenance schedules and a trouble-shooting section for my car. So does my physician – colonoscopy, mammograms, prostate checks for men, and breast exams for women. For example, women are instructed to examine their breasts monthly, but are they informed of problems that can occur when estrogen levels drop prior to menses, which may affect their serotonin levels? Are they chastised by family and friends for their "moodiness"? Do they feel guilty because they are less patient with their children? Education can do wonders in preventing that needle on the 'self-esteem monitor' from dipping too low.

I am a Psychiatrist. I really don't have that luxury to poke and prod or just plug you in. I am dependent on clients sensing that something is wrong mentally. This is not an easy thing for individuals to do. I can't lift up the cranium and exam the brain. And the last time I looked at my laboratory request for blood work, there were no detectors for depression, anxiety, OCD – well you get my concerns.

There are many reasons that I never see individuals in my office. The primary one is the stigma of mental illness. Too often the yellow light is on its way to red, an almost orange, if you will. And the red light folks most often are seen in an ER and/or hospitalized.

Unfortunately, I never see a patient who presents for the first time with mild depressive symptoms. They may blame Cleveland weather or chalk it up to "I've been this way all my life." And God forbid if I ever, ever see a hypomanic patient in my office. Those individuals have increased energy, euphoria, feel some empowerment, and are too busy enjoying the multiple home-shopping purchases made at 3 A.M. With food tasting better, roses smelling sweeter, and a heightened sense of confidence, do you honestly think that any of these individuals come to me asking, "Doc, snap me out of this!"

So the purpose of this book, taking all of the above concerns into consideration, is an attempt to put the brakes on any emerging problems and address all the yellow lights that may appear on our dashboard. As you see, I am speaking in metaphors. And in doing so, I have found it a more effective way in explaining our own engine or biological parts.

Also, what makes some of us better able to manipulate the steering wheel? I am addressing our coping mechanisms, our ability to process and to react to and handle situations.

And why do some journeys create more difficulty for some vehicles than others? In other words, the social stressors we face can certainly affect the way we drive, asking us to maneuver some situations we may not be prepared to navigate. The dashboard may light up like a Christmas tree!

And most importantly, I want to introduce the concept of Mental Wellness, not Illness. Why can't we have an understanding of how our own body operates, how we normally interact with others, or how we cope with stressors? Why can't we learn to be more anticipatory about a future event that usually repeats itself in less desirable outcomes? Here's an example. Maybe you are dreading the holidays because "My family is so dysfunctional. We always end up fighting." But before you drove over the river and through the woods to grandmother's house, I'll bet you checked your tire pressure and changed the oil in your car. What did you do to identify patterns of behaviors that tend to repeat themselves in family situations? How prepared were you? See, you may be taking better care of your car than yourself.

With the following chapters in this book I will provide education about our biological and psychological designs and how our social environment can influence them. We will develop our own internal yellow light system, if you will. My goal is to help you recognize those signs and symptoms that could indicate an impending problem, making you aware of your own inner dashboard.

I feel obligated to first offer a disclaimer at this point. This book is in no way dismissing the seriousness of mental illness. As a psychiatrist, I have treated the severely depressed, lost patients to suicide, struggled with patients not taking their medications because "the voices" told them not to, and witnessed individuals lose jobs, lose spouses, and lose their rightful place in society because of unmanaged mania, panic attacks, and substance abuse.

I know these patients well, and they first come to my office when they can no longer deal with their symptoms, when their family forced them to get help, or when a psychiatric admission or judge has required them to see me for an assessment or follow-up.

So, how do circumstances evolve in individuals where a decline in function, apparent often to others but not themselves, require them to seek treatment? Insurance companies are on top of the game. Unless you are suicidal, homicidal, or clearly failing to take care of yourself that presents imminent danger to your health, admission to a psychiatric ward can be very discriminatory. And length of stay for a patient is often not measured in the patient's best interest but rather in the cost benefit to the institution.

Having said all of this, I will not take on the politics of mental illness at this time. I have seen major hospitals in my hometown move their psychiatric facilities off campus. They do not generate the income other medical specialties do. Ah, another slap in psychiatry's face. And forget the way the media portray the mentally ill. My clients are often introduced to psychiatry through Hollywood's eyes. A common question when I suggest a medication is, "Will I look like a zombie?"

But soon, I do hope that with improved education, which includes respecting mental disorders and substance abuse as true illnesses, we will slowly begin to reverse the stigmatization of these individuals.

So, we will take this journey together to understand how we all arrived at our current mental functioning. How we have taken care of our engine and our chassis since birth has had a number of influencing factors. The biological influences, the psychological influences, and the social influences will remain an integral part of each discussion.

I have just one request before we proceed. In this book we will learn how to care for ourselves. We will be prepared for those long car journeys. If you happen to carry a blanket in your car just in case you are stranded in a snowstorm, please keep an extra blanket on hand. And if you happen to pass by a homeless person, please offer them this simple gift. It will not only warm them, but will also warm your heart.

Introduction:
The Car, The Drive, The Journey
or
"Our Very own GPS System"

Should I begin this introduction with another disclaimer? I think I should. I am not a car mechanic. Never have been. I do know that I was born with this specific engine and chassis. How I choose and continue to care for it is up to my mechanical skills. That is where the car mechanic and I part company.

I feel very confident in discussing what lies under my hood. Having "driven" or lived in this chassis since birth (well – 61 years to date), I have chalked up millions of miles on my odometer. I cannot trade me in. I own this car for life.

There were some initial guidelines in my owner's manual. As a child, my parents took me to Dr. Lace for the obligatory immunizations. As medicine became more enlightened and began to emphasize preventative guidelines, my glove compartment became stuffed with further instructions.

Family history also began to play a more important role. Not only was the color of my chassis determined by them, but also the possibility of developing other unique options not apparent at birth or in my early years of traveling. This is the biological influence on my car's design. Psychological development and social factors would play an important role in whether these options would later appear. My car was assembled in Tarentum, Pennsylvania by the Arnold-Campbell manufacturing company.

In addition, my ability to navigate life's path was either enhanced or exacerbated by my driving skills. How did my car respond to the road? Did my tires meet the pavement and hug every curve or did I insist I owned the entire road? Was I courteous to others, behaving like a peaceful dove, or did I find myself flicking the dove when someone cut me off? Was I a safe driver, or did I take risks? How many traffic tickets did I accumulate? Oh, I could go on and on, but I think you get my gist. Our driving skills are directly related to our psychological makeup. How were we taught to "drive" or to cope as we progressed down life's highway? Our coping skills are a direct function of our unique psychological makeup, or our personality, our mood du jour, on how we perceive the world through our headlights.

And finally, the road itself is never guaranteed to be a smooth one. We all drive an obstacle course, unique to our own lives. Looking back on your own journey, can you identify specific trips that were straight from the streets of 'H-E- double hockey sticks'? Every turn out of our driveway has managed to impact us in either a positive or in a negative way. The outcome of the journey really depends on the combination of all of the above.

So, what am I driving at? Our biological makeup with its family history, our ability to drive, and our obstacle courses make us all completely different. Yes, even identical twins, born with identical genetic chasses and engines, will be affected by these factors. Psychiatry refers to this as the Biopsychosocial impact. This very important word is underscored in red on my computer. Why? I have my spell check on. But I would love to believe that it is underlined because of its significance on our lives, not that this stupid computer dismisses it as not existing. And, if you are willing to accept that your initial biological makeup is your genetic makeup, then I will change the "Bio" to "Genetic" and will rename it as the GeneticPsychoSocial impact on our lives. Oops. The dang computer still refuses to recognize this word. But my metaphor is intact. We have a GPS system unique to us all.

So, allow me to be your guide through the genetic, psychological, and social aspects that have created the wonderful person who is reading this manual. Shall we start our journey? And don't cheat by jumper cabling to Part 3. We need to be familiar with the car, the accessories, and do a bit of a maintenance check-up before we hit the road, right? So let's get started!

Part One

The Car
or
"The Biological Engine"

Chapter I

Your Brain
or
"You Want to Look Under My Hood?"

I can't help but recall a question asked of me by a young child undergoing an MRI. She gazed up into my eyes as I was preparing to inject her with some Gadolinium for contrast. You might be wondering at this point why a Psychiatrist was in an MRI suite. Well I began my residency training in Radiology at University Hospitals prior to switching into Psychiatry. I will never regret the knowledge I gained in my residencies.

Sorry. Let's get back to the story. She asked me a question I never suspected, but understanding the stages of development in childhood and the magical thinking that occurs during that time, it now makes sense. She was concerned about her private thoughts and her own magical world that she had created in her mind. "Will anyone be able to see my thoughts or my wishes?" I smiled at her and reassured her that an MRI can only look at the structures in her brain. Her personal space and her private thoughts and wishes would not show up on the screen. She was the only one who had the key to unlock them. And that key for all of us is the ability to verbally communicate our thoughts and our feelings to others.

The point that I am attempting to make is that we are all more than the sum of the parts of our brain. Our perceptions, our thoughts, our feelings, and the complexity of these forces on influencing the way we behave are not physical entities but ongoing dynamic ones.

In my attempt to better explain myself as a car-mechanic-psychiatric specialist, I ran across a staggering statistic. Did you know that if you looked under your car's hood 15 minutes per month – and that just isn't staring at the engine – you might prevent 70% of car troubles that might lead to further break-downs? That is just not acceptable to me. We need to take better care of ourselves than we do our cars. To date, I have googled and researched high and low for a statistic that might refer to a percentage on how fewer breakdowns would occur in humans if they would only take a few minutes each month to look under their own hood – to decompress, to relax, and to assess their stress level. I have found none to date. Well, we end that nonsense right now. Let's take a look, shall we?

First of all, there is a thing-a-ma-jig under your dashboard that releases the hood. If you would kindly release it for me, then we can open the hood and see what we have here. You see psychiatry is a very confidential practice. Furthermore, it is very important that you trust and feel confident with your mechanic, i.e., psychiatrist.

Otherwise, we will go no further. What good have I served you if you put this book down, never to make another checkup with me again?

Well, silly me. We can't really look under your cranium can we? So for the purpose of maintaining my metaphors, your thing-a-ma-jig is stuck. Or you just can't find that release hook that the mechanic can easily find to lift the hood. So allow me to be your guide to what lies beneath. Trust me, I know what lies in that noggin of yours. I dissected the brain in medical school, and I saw the beautiful structures outlined in MRI's.

We will begin with the engine, or your brain. Just as there are many parts to the engine, there are more than equivalent parts to the brain.

Your brain came fully assembled the day you were born. It may not be as shiny and new but that is to be expected as we age. And, hopefully, it purrs like a kitten. Not to worry if it doesn't. We will examine problems that can affect the way the brain operates in later chapters. For example, muffler issues (not directly visible when looking at the brain but embedded in our limbic system) can affect our moods and the way we are perceived by others. "My, your voice sounds as if you are angry." Or better said, "You loud mouth!" Battery issues can affect your energy. Are you a couch potato? Spark plugs can motivate you. Up to date with paying bills?

Anyway, the complexity of the engine or brain requires separate chapters devoted to its overall operation.

When I refer to the brain, I am referring to the electrical system in your car. And that is exactly how the brain communicates. Its cells, called neurons, fire an electrical potential that can be detected by an EEG.

And just as there are sensors in our car, our brain is dependent upon its own sensors as well. How could we have survived as a species if we did not have the capacity to know when to drink when we were thirsty, to hunt for game when we were hungry, and to derive pleasure from sex to procreate and prevent extinction? Do we not put jammies on at night when we feel tired?

I have mentioned EEG's and MRI's, haven't I? These wonderful tests can actually detect physiological problems in the brain. An EEG, for example, can determine if an individual's electrical system is intact. Epilepsy can be diagnosed. Brain death is verified if no electrical activity is present.

Because MRI's can detail the structures of the brain; tumors, infections, strokes, multiple sclerosis, aneurisms, etc., can be detected.

More recent neuroimaging or brain scans has permitted researchers and clinicians to detect patterns in the structure of the brain that are more likely seen in certain mental conditions. For example, individuals with certain types of dementia may have less volume in the frontal area of the brain that controls executive function and enables me to act like a lady when out in public. Pick's disease, a certain type of dementia, normally shows decreased volume or activity in the frontal lobe on brain scans. As a result of this volume loss, inability to balance checkbooks is lost. Disinhibition occurs as well. Ladylike behaviors are no longer observed in public.

However, to date, there are no brain scans available to diagnosis a mental illness or to predict the probability of developing an illness such as depression, anxiety disorders, bipolar disorder, schizophrenia, or alcohol or drug addiction.

This makes psychiatry a unique field of medicine. The brain alone does not make up our disorders. Otherwise, they would be detected on imaging. We could just plug in to the contraption, and that particular car mechanic, or radiologist, would diagnosis the problem.

Here is an example. You had a headache for weeks and it has affected your functioning. Migraines have been ruled out. Your doctor orders an MRI. Why? Obviously to rule out any physiological changes that could account for your pain. It comes back normal. Now what? Have you ever been insulted by your physician when he requests that you see a Psychiatrist? "What do you mean that this is all in my head?" I have heard this complaint so often by those few who actually do follow their physician's advice and come to see me for an assessment.

Imaging will not detect your coping mechanisms. Our personality isn't located in the coronal view on T2 weighted imaging. Sorry. My radiology days were showing weren't they? And the miserable life you are leading with a boss from hell, a family waiting at home for dinner, and the bills piling up is just not blinking on the MRI screen either.

So how do we fix those parts of the brain that are affecting your ability to perceive a situation, affecting the way you think, the way you feel, and the way you behave?

As your car mechanic/psychiatric guru, it is my job to navigate you through some of the possible glitches in the works.

Shall we do some more exploring?

Chapter 2

Your Neurotransmitters
or
"Reading the Dipstick"

Have you ever learned how to check your oil level? I was so proud of myself when I located the dipstick. I removed it, cleaned it off, and dipped it in again. Aha! Low on oil. Yellow lights hadn't gone off on the dash, but looking at the old odometer, I had put on a few thousand miles and, for maintenance sake, thought I would check.

Oil is absolutely essential for the smooth operation of your car. And likewise, neurotransmitters are necessary for the neurons to communicate with one another in your brain, resulting in a happy, purring engine up there. But this is not always so. Unfortunately we have no dipstick to warn us of impending problems. However, I promise you, that by the end of this chapter, you will be familiar with some of your neurotransmitters. You may also identify some impending yellow lights or actually admit that one is flashing on your dashboard. You see, some symptoms you might be experiencing could be indicating that an oil check is in order.

So the first thing I want to discuss with you is the fluids or neurotransmitters that are responsible for the way neurons communicate with each other.

The oil level in your car I equate to the neurotransmitters in your brain. I will concentrate on serotonin, norepinephrine, dopamine, and gabapentin, specifically, as these four fluids require adequate balances for smooth operation. In other words, how your car operates on the highway or how it never wants to leave the dang garage can be partially related to the balance of neurotransmitters in the engine. So, let's take a closer look.

Serotonin is responsible for mood regulation, such as depression and irritability. In addition it reduces anxiety, obsessive thoughts, and compulsive behaviors. Serotonin agents are called SSRI's, meaning selective serotonin reuptake inhibitors. Serotonin, as well as other neurotransmitters is released into a junction in between neurons, enabling them to communicate with one another and thus help the brain operate smoothly. If serotonin levels are low, any of the above symptoms can be experienced. Serotonin cannot cross the blood brain barrier, so these agents were designed to work within the brain to increase the amount of serotonin in the synapse or junction between the neurons.

Since birth, your brain has been a big recycler, as far as preserving some neurotransmitters. Little vesicles pick up the serotonin after release into that junction. It then returns that precious serotonin back into the neuron that just released it for future use. Well, SSRI's prevent the reuptake process by throwing a good wrench into the works by blocking the transporter that was returning it to the neuron. As a result, more serotonin is available in the junction, and symptoms such as those listed above can be alleviated. Examples of Serotonin drugs include Prozac, Paxil, Celexa, Lexapro, Luvox, and Zoloft.

So, if my client complains of depression, irritability, ruminative thoughts, and anxiety, my first assessment is that a lower serotonin level might be contributing to these symptoms. My dipstick or diagnostic assessment is measuring the fluid level through symptom retrieval from the client. A trial of a serotonin agent can, often times, improve these symptoms.

And as I mentioned earlier, I have noticed that in some females, there is increased irritability and mood changes when estrogen levels drop. In these individuals, there seems to be a dysfunction between serotonin and estrogen. Adding or increasing an SSRI approximately one week before the onset of menses and continuing the dose for two to three more days often times relieves these symptoms. This drop in estrogen also occurs after giving birth, putting some women at risk for developing post-partum depression.

Now, if my client complains of difficulty concentrating with depressive symptoms present, including anhedonia, or lack of pleasure, I consider an agent that contains norepinephrine. Again, listening closely to the client's complaints can offer an inside view, very informally, of the levels of certain neurotransmitters. Agents containing norepinephrine are usually combined with serotonin. They, again, work by recycling the neurotransmitter as described above. These medications include Remeron – a great choice if insomnia is a problem, Effexor, Cymbalta, and Pristiq, with Pristiq and Effexor also having an ability to capture dopamine activity as well.

For all of my couch potatoes that have no energy, no longer enjoy their car trips, and have more complaints of depression than anxiety, with difficulty focusing and poor motivation, I often prescribe a dopamine agent. I often prescribe Wellbutrin for these individuals. Wellbutrin provides increased dopamine action. Dopamine is a neurotransmitter that improves attention. It activates my clients to get off the couch and get in that car. That is why it is always given in the morning. It is always a joy when clients return to my office and say, "I think we found the right med, Doc."

Dopamine is a fascinating and complicated neurotransmitter, because it has different functions in the brain. It can stimulate or inhibit certain functions. For instance, many of my adult clients present to me with complaints of attention-deficit. They miss their exit and they cannot focus on the road ahead. Now here is where I am thankful for my exposure to neuroimaging during my radiology days. Studies have suggested that the brains of children with ADHD differ from other children. Some of the neurotransmitters which we have discussed, specifically dopamine and serotonin, as well as adrenalin are handled differently by these children. Most adults admit that their symptoms of inattentiveness and/or hyperactivity were present as a child but that the school lacked a psychologist or their parents tolerated their behaviors. If I am certain that my client has ADD or ADHD I prescribe a psychostimulant such as Adderall or Ritalin. The diagnosis is clinched when they return with tears of joy saying, "Is this the way life was meant to be?!" If the medication causes no improvement, I search for other diagnoses.

Dopamine's role in providing pleasure was critical for our initial survival and, therefore, was connected to a reward system in our brains. As I discussed before, we felt a sense of joy when we ate or had sex. Otherwise, the species, without food or procreation, would have become extinct. I will admit that something goes on up there in my brain when I eat chocolate chip cookies or potato chips. I can't stop! Oh, and I used to love a good champagne. As a result, behaviors that lead to a release of dopamine from the reward center, such as consumption of alcohol, marijuana, cocaine, strong pain medication such as Percocet, or benzodiazepines such as Valium, are likely to be reinforced and may lead to addiction. A history of alcohol and drug use in my clients is an essential part of the initial interview. If your car's gas gauge is always reading "way over full", you may be a gas-guzzler. We definitely need to talk.

I love to pull out of the mechanic's garage after my car had a tune up. I notice the difference. I cannot promise my clients the same experience. On average it may take two weeks and as long as four weeks for any of the above medication to begin to improve symptoms. Medication such as Adderall, or Valium, a benzodiazepine affecting gabapentin activity, will act almost immediately.

This is where education comes in. If you expected results right away from the above medications and were not prepared with possible side effects, including weight gain and sexual side effects, I guarantee that you would either never pull into my garage again or at least lose faith entirely in your medication. After all, when you had a headache, you would go to your medicine cabinet, take two tablets of your favorite over-the-counter pain reliever and expect results within fifteen to thirty minutes. And there are actually individuals handed an anti-depressant that were not forewarned of the time needed to wait for a response. They assume it is ineffective and either place a phone call to their clinician with complaints or flush it down the toilet. How unfortunate.

I mentioned weight gain, didn't I? Well, as I stated earlier, knowledge is power. I often learn, after talking to my clients, that their perception of the medication is that it contains several calories. When I inform them that the pill is "0 calories" and that perhaps we need to look at their own eating habits, I either get a litany of denials that any change in food intake has occurred or demands to be taken off a medication that has actually been effective. Food journaling is a good thing. More importantly, knowing their family's medical history, including diabetes and obtaining blood work to monitor blood sugars and to rule out hypothyroidism is just good medical practice.

Talk, talk, talk to your clients! Sorry this last statement isn't meant for you. It is meant to serve as a reminder to some of my colleagues.

And let's talk about the biggest hurdle I face when suggesting medication. "I have been told that this medication will make me want to drive my car into Lake Erie." Yes, there has been much negative press about the side effects of some anti-depressants and their increasing suicidal thoughts in a small percentage of teens. Read that again, an increase in suicidal thoughts – not in suicide rate. The study focused on teens and as a result of the study, the FDA put a warning on all SSRI's that this unwanted side effect may occur. It should also have been a reminder to providers to weigh the pros and cons and increase their vigil of the client, and not to serve as a scare tactic to them along with their patient.

Now I applaud any car manufacturer that recalls a car for a defective part. But the actions of the FDA actually influenced a great many psychiatrists to back away from prescribing SSRI's to depressed teens. As a result, the suicide rate of teens has now increased. Many have blamed the FDA for scaring not only clients but also providers in this very litigious society. My philosophy is always to do what I feel is best for my client. I took my oath seriously at my medical school graduation, "To do no harm."

Since we are speaking of biological influences, many individuals have had the inheritance deck stacked against them and may have defective parts. Their car could have been assembled with parts that are more inclined to breakdown with improper care. For example, you have a history of alcoholism in your family, you throw caution to the wind and decide to party, party, party, and your chances of being in a ditch on the road, unable to get out, are much improved. Part 2 and Part 3 will examine how psychological makeup and social stressors respectively can impact our genetic makeup and result in development of symptoms and/or a disorder.

So, I have given you an introduction to some of the neurotransmitters of the brain and how they can bring on certain symptoms. I even went so far as discussing the medication or DW40's that might be recommended for smooth operation.

Now it is time to further exam your vehicle. We shall look at some of those other pieces of equipment that help you become the driver that you are.

Just how accessorized are you?

Chapter 3

Your Hypothalamus
or
"Do I Need Jumper Cables, New Spark Plugs, or is My Tank Empty?"

The hypothalamus is a very small but extremely important part of our brain. As part of our engine, it controls the temperature of your car, letting you know when it is overheating. It also senses when we need to fuel up. And, just as important, it tells us when to put the car in the garage to rest.

In this chapter, we will equate the hypothalamus to the battery, spark plugs, radiator, and gas tank.

Did you know that some individuals who might be suffering from a psychiatric problem only admit to the physical or medical changes they experience? "I haven't been sleeping well." "My energy level is low, and I feel so fatigued." "My appetite has changed." These physiological symptoms that are expressed by patients may be impending yellow warning lights. Mood and anxiety disorders may have sleep and appetite disturbances. Low energy may be experienced by individuals suffering from depression or seasonal affective changes. So naturally it is important to address these concerns before leaving the biological section.

Now, there are days I just don't want to get out of bed. Maybe menopause has finally caught up with me – a biological influence. It could be that I dread what I need to do that day – a possible stressor interfering with sleep. Maybe my mind would not shut off before I finally caught some shuteye – requiring further investigation to rule out possible psychological reasons.

Sleep can certainly affect our energy levels. And I guarantee that if lack of sleep is due to poor sleep hygiene – caffeine or nicotine close to be bedtime, Internet surfing, or watching TV in bed – no yellow light will appear. The cure is to adapt good sleep habits. For example, if you are waking up to urinate frequently throughout the night, please examine your evening liquid consumption. The bladder is a powerful "waker-upper," so no water after 8 P.M. Nighttime meds should be taken with just a sip of water. Bed is just for sex and sleeping. If you cannot fall asleep within twenty minutes, get up, sit in a chair, and read until you feel tired. No caffeine or nicotine late at night – it is a stimulant.

Now, if you do not fall under the poor sleep hygiene category and you are a male that wakes up because of the need to urinate frequently, please make sure you have an appointment with your doctor to rule out any prostate problems. This is a biological problem affecting your sleep.

Perimenopausal females experience hot flashes, premeno-pausal would not but some are unaware of the effect it has on normal sleep patterns.

And individuals who are obese can be prone to developing obstructive sleep apnea – a condition where added pressure on the soft tissues of the neck can actually cause a collapse in the windpipe, causing lack of oxygen to the brain. The brain, being the survivor that it is, nudges you out of the restful sleep into a more restless state to get you back on track. A nudge from your spouse to roll over will also help, but a sleep study is in order to rule out this condition.

Yes, a lack of sleep can cause decreased energy. However, so can thyroid issues or anemia.

And what about appetite changes? Our gas tank may be empty, and yet we cannot fill it up. Have you ever lost your appetite or actually noticed an increase in appetite causing a five percent change in weight in a four-week period of time?

Weight changes can be a warning sign that something physio-logical is going on. If any of my clients complain of weight loss without any significant psychiatric symptoms, I become concerned that a medical problem might be the cause. If they are a smoker, I send them for a chest x-ray. I consider thyroid problems or diabetic issues and obtain lab work.

I have discussed some medical reasons that can alter sleep, affect energy levels, or cause weight loss or gain. If you follow up on a regular basis with your physician, then some of these causes may be detected through simple lab tests.

Psychological conditions can also affect your sleep, appetite, and energy level. For instance, depression, bipolar disorder, anxiety, post-traumatic stress disorder, and excessive alcohol consumption all share insomnia, as well as appetite and energy level changes, as symptoms. As I mentioned above, if my coping skills are not up to par and my day is full of stressors, then I may want to pull those sheets over my head. We may all have days like that. But most of us manage to shake it off and do what we have to do. We sharpen our coping mechanisms and assess the significance of the stressor that day. If we survive it, we feel a sense of accomplishment and perhaps an improved mood.

The yellow light will definitely turn on should any of these symptoms persist and begin to affect your ability to function.

Other symptoms may also be present. Repeatedly calling in to cancel work, or not getting up to get the kids off to school may indicate something more serious is present. For instance, you may be depressed. We will look at the collection of symptoms necessary to make this diagnosis, as well as others in the following chapters.

Part Two

The Drive
or
"Your Psychological Parts and Accessories"

Chapter 4

The Steering Wheel
or
"How Are My Driving Skills?"

We have devoted the first part of this book to understanding some of the basic components of our engine that can have a biological influence on us. Now we will inspect other components of our car that can affect us in a more psychological way. You see, the car doesn't drive by itself. It takes a driver to operate that steering wheel. What type of driver are you?

First of all, I have a confession to make. Because this chapter is devoted to the person behind the wheel and how our moods, our psychological makeup, can affect our driving habits, I must share this story. Now promise that you won't think any less of your car mechanic/psychiatric guru who wants to enlighten you, not to scare you away.

I was on my way to work. Was I a little late? I don't think so but the person ahead of me was not turning left when the green arrow appeared. And I do believe I gave him adequate time before I beeped at him. You think I had learned my lesson from a previous warning offered to me by my son. I was picking him up from college years ago and was traveling through, how shall I describe this, "Deliverance" country. I beeped at a man in a pickup truck for thinking that he owned the bleeping road. Well, Peter grabbed my right hand, turned pale, and said, "Mom, you don't beep at people in pickup trucks in this neck of the woods – they carry!" Carry what, I wondered? Rifles!

Back to the story. Yes the man was in a pickup truck, but it was all shiny and new and not rusted and appearing like it was just taken off the cinder blocks in the backyard. And toward my left I could see my favorite shopping plaza. I was in a lovely neighborhood. So imagine my surprise when this jerk flips me the bird. And to make sure I saw it, he rolls down his window on that frosty December morn and holds his arm out to continue flipping me, just in case I missed it the first time.

Well. I can recall other times when I have met his cousins on the road and have received the same greeting. I would feel the shame and, of course, the fear immediately. I permitted these jerks to completely ruin a perfectly nice ride in my car.

Then I met Jerry, a wonderful therapist, who taught me a wonderful mantra to repeat to myself should someone's behavior affect me like this. "Whatever so and so thinks, says, or does is more a reflection of them than of you. And whatever you think, say, or do is more a reflection of you." Sounds quite simple, doesn't it? But boy does it work. It seems to put things more in perspective, at least for me it does. And here is why.

As the jerk is freezing his arm off as it hangs out the window, and I am secretly hoping that his middle finger gets frostbite, I don't cower. I don't slow down and avoid him. Oh no. That mantra is playing in my head and I decide to pull up alongside of him – it was a four-laner, and I had the golden opportunity to keep pace with him. I actually made eye contact with him, and, rather puzzled, he pulls in his arm but continues his attempt to shame me at a less intense level. He frowns. First of all, I noted that the poor man could have used some botox. The frown brought out some terrible deep wrinkles in his glabellar region. I continued to gaze at him. He now is looking a bit demoralized. Who knows what he was thinking? "This used to work before." "Who IS this crazy woman?" I smiled at him and then did something I never thought I would ever do. I blew him a kiss. Quite the opposite gesture that he afforded me just moments ago. Well – I never saw someone veer to the brim and speed their way to the next intersection. As I proceeded on my way, I could see the tire marks on the road as he made his next turn as if he were in the Indy 500. Thank you, Jerry!

I am in no way endorsing this behavior. Heavens no! Like Peter warned me, he could have been carrying. However, my mood was different. I was empowered. I was not personally offended by his gesture. I did feel sorry for others who may not have known that the little birdie was meant for me (and possibly for them) and began to alter their own driving habits at that moment.

The chapters in Part 2 are dealing with our psychological makeup. What parts of the car are involved? Several. I may be the driver manipulating the steering wheel but my eyes, or headlights, and the clarity of my windshield (which by the way gave me a clear view of the jerk) feed into the electrical system of my car, and caused me to react to this gesture. In other words, we process our environment with all of our senses. Our brain then interprets them. Example – I'm flipped the bird; I feel ashamed or angry or both.

My behavior is expressed through a variety of elements in the interior of my car -my gas pedal, my brake, my horn (in this scenario), and my steering wheel. How did my feelings, processed by the perception I had of this jerk, affect my behavior? Well, I could have cringed. Done that. I could have flipped him back. I think I have done that. I could have blown my horn again to anger him more. Definitely have done that, and this is not recommended. Or I could have surprised myself, done a 180, and blown a kiss. Done that with surprising results.

Part 1 dealt with the brain, the neurotransmitters and the hypothalamus that are just a few anatomical parts responsible for the biological operation of our engine. We also discussed some of the physiological changes that may occur to affect our sleep, appetite and energy levels. Now we will look at how our psychological makeup has just as much effect on that dashboard.

Ever make a quick observation of the cars that surround you on the highway? They come in a variety of makes, models, colors, and conditions. How boring the drive if cars similar to mine surrounded me. Yes, I would appreciate them all having the most considerate of drivers behind the wheel, but that is what makes life so interesting, doesn't it? And sometimes I learn just as much about myself as I do the other drivers by observing their habits.

When I refer to habits, I am actually referring to the personality of the driver. Our personalities are all unique, made up of a set of emotional qualities that affect the way we behave behind the wheel.

The psychological makeup of all of us is a process that involves so many factors. If you were to study psychology in school, you would be familiar with names such as Freud, Erikson, and Piaget. All of these famous psychiatrists or psychologists developed their own theories on different stages of development and how it forms our psychological makeup. For instance, Jean Piaget felt that Trust vs. Mistrust was an important milestone from birth through one year. If you were nurtured and your needs were met, you would move on to Autonomy vs. Shame and Doubt, coinciding with preschool years. Children should be encouraged to do what they are capable of doing with proper supervision from the parent.

I am just emphasizing that all of what we experience as we grow up in this world has a strong influence on how we perceive our environment. How we perceive things impacts how we think and how we feel. And how we feel definitely influences our behavior doesn't it? Our personalities evolve, and our coping mechanisms are very much influenced by our uniqueness. How would you describe your personality?

In psychiatry, we have a manual that enables us to make proper diagnoses, whether it is mood, anxiety, or psychotic disorders, to name a few.

With regard to personality, there are ten disorders. These personality disorders are "inflexible and pervasive." This behavior can result in the individual adopting maladaptive coping skills. These personality problems can cause anxiety, depression, and much distress in these particular drivers.

My favorite way of understanding personality disorders is to observe the way these individuals park their cars in a lot.

The Paranoid Personality would insist to the attendant that his car was purposely blocked in by other cars. "I've been trapped!"

The Narcissist can be easily spotted. He or she usually owns the largest car in the lot with a very fancy hood ornament or other distinguishing feature. "Look at me. I am very important."

The Borderline Personality is the individual that just rammed her ex-lover's car and slashed his tires. "How dare you abandon me, you son of a female dog!"

The Anti-Social Personality will just go ahead and double-park, not caring if he blocks you in or not. "I don't give a #$%*!" Also, have you ever wondered who is parked in the handicapped space illegally?

The Dependent Personality will try to squeeze next to you in your parking place. "I feel better when I have you near."

The Histrionic Personality will park the car in the middle of the lot, not in the designated areas, just for dramatic effects. "I am such a Drama Queen."

The Obsessive-Compulsive Personality will park the car in perfect alignment from front to back and side to side. Sorry to say that he is still parking the car.

The Avoidant Personality Disorder hides the car in the farthest corner of the lot. "Do I have to come out of this car and do what I have to do?"

The Schizoid Personality Disorder who can't tolerate being near any individual will make his own spot halfway off the lot. "I hate being around those other cars."

The Schizotypal Personality can be spotted with an inter-galactic vehicle. "People think I am a bit odd. I am just a bit eccentric."

The Passive-Aggressive individual is not formally diagnosed as a disorder but certainly has traits and can be spotted by the way the car is angled to take up two spaces, "not really meaning to." If my client and I had a difficult session at our last appointment, they may show up late for the next one.

Now, again, I want to emphasize that I am not making light of personality disorders. As I mentioned above, these disorders can lead to a miserable life because of their inability to deal with life. They have maladaptive coping mechanisms. And it also can make life difficult for those who have to deal with these individuals, either in family situations, the workplace, or on the highway.

We all may possess some of the above traits. It is when these traits become so rigid and inflexible and become the preferred way that they park their car that a personality disorder emerges.

Well, whether it is traits or a disorder, we all have our own unique way of interacting with the world.

Now it's time take a look at our coping mechanisms.

Chapter 5

The Gearbox
or
"How Well Are You Geared-up for the Trip?"

In the previous chapter we explored personality disorders, which are some of the maladaptive driving forces behind these individuals that effect their thoughts, feelings, and actions, over and over again.

Now we will look at the defense mechanisms that we all have developed since childhood. I have repeatedly discussed the importance that our childhood experiences and its influence have on our psychological development. Our coping skills are very much related to just how effective and "geared up" our defense mechanisms are.

Defense mechanisms are fairly unconscious. They represent our mannerisms. They influence how we think, how we feel, how we behave, and control some of our impulsive behaviors.

Psychologists have categorized fifteen defense mechanisms into three groups. I will begin to describe the Primitive defenses, which I equate to being in Reverse. Primitive defense mechanisms do little to try and resolve underlying issues or problems.

The next grouping is the Less Primitive and More Mature defense mechanisms. We have gone from Park into Neutral, still able to fend off those unwanted feeling and impulses, but still not necessarily enjoying the ride quite yet. We may manage to get into first gear, but sounds to me like the engine is struggling a bit.

And, finally (oh, PLEASE let me see myself in this grouping), I list the Mature defense mechanisms. Mature defenses are more focused on helping a person be more effective and constructive in dealing with their environment. The car is in Drive and these individuals are able to enjoy those car rides with a sense of peace and well-being.

Let's take a look at those defense mechanisms. The importance of doing so will help you identify the methods you might use when faced with an uncomfortable situation, thought, feeling, or impulse. The more we understand about ourselves, the better able we can engage into a different gear. You see, defense mechanisms are not personality disorders. They are not so ingrained and maladaptive that you cannot challenge them or substitute more healthy ones. I will never get to where I am going stuck in Park, Neutral, or, God forbid, Reverse.

Primitive Defense Mechanisms:

1) Denial – You absolutely refuse to accept a thought or feeling that you are not able to tolerate. You reject it. This is very characteristic of childhood development. Although you might feel angry with someone, you reject the thought. "I am not angry." I have seen this defense used in my clients with alcohol and drug dependence. "I only drink on weekends." "I go to work every day – I am functioning quite well, thank you."

2) Regression – You put yourself in reverse, literally. You return to an earlier way of dealing with an unacceptable thought or feeling. For instance, a teen may revert to bedwetting. An adult may refuse to leave bed. The comforter serves as a baby blanket as you cling to it, unable to get up and face the day.

3) Acting-Out – This defense uses an extreme behavior to express an unwanted thought or feeling. In children it is viewed as a temper-tantrum. In adults, some individuals choose to punch a wall or, unfortunately, superficially cut their forearm. It serves as a short-term fix for their anger but does

nothing long term to address it. You are stuck in neutral. You will never move forward unless you allow yourself to deal with the discomfort of the situation in more healthy ways.

4) Dissociation – This is a very primitive defense mechanism where individuals lose track of time and often themselves. They place themselves in a less threatening world when overcome with unpleasant thoughts, feelings, or actions against them. I have seen many of my clients with childhood abuse, especially molestation, that present with this coping style. Can you imagine as a young, defenseless child, being forced by an adult, usually a family member or neighbor, to perform sexual acts against your will? You are threatened, and you are demeaned. Some of these unfortunate children can only cope by shutting off their minds at this time. They dissociate to a field of sunflowers or imagine themselves as a different person. There is no gear for this. Children scarred by these criminal acts have difficulty in later life with trust issues. Can you blame them? And they will still often use this very immature defense mechanism to put a safety net around them.

5) Compartmentalization – This is a less severe form of dissociation. These individuals seem to have two sets of values that are kept separate from one another. There is no conscious awareness of this. For instance, one may claim and believe oneself to be the most honest person in the world but does not think twice about cheating on a test.

6) Projection – You refuse to accept your own thoughts or feelings and ascribe them to another. You may be angry that someone is not listening to you, when it is you that is not listening. This defense mechanism demonstrates a lack of insight and the inability to acknowledge one's own feelings or motivation.

7) Reaction Formation - This defense mechanism converts our unwanted thoughts and feelings into the exact opposite. For instance, you may hate your job or despise your boss. You are unable to express that, so you do a 180 and are overly sweet and friendly to your boss and co-workers.

Now we move on to describe more mature defense mechanisms. Let's move into some gear that can get us moving!

8) Repression /Suppression– Repression is the mother of all defense mechanisms, so they say. It deals with the unconscious blocking of unacceptable thoughts, feelings, or impulses. These are stored in the memory bank and are not retrieved. However, they are still present. For instance, we formerly discussed childhood abuse. This experience is buried so to speak. However, this unconscious memory may still be responsible for the individual's inability to form healthy relationships later in life. As repression is an unconscious blocking, suppression is the conscious blocking of unwanted thoughts and impulses. In other words, I may be vaguely aware of the thought or feeling, but I really try to hide it. "I will try to be nice."

9) Displacement – This defense mechanism is very well named. We redirect our thoughts, feelings or impulses to another person or object. You had a miserable day at the office. You were angry with the boss, but were unable to express it. You come home and pick an argument with your wife. Worse yet, you may kick the dog. (Sorry, I did not mean to imply that an argument with a spouse is less harmful. I am a huge animal lover, that's all.) This defense mechanism is ineffective because the misdirection of anger can cause further problems such as marital discourse.

10) Intellectualization – You overthink everything. God forbid if you have a manual transmission, because you would be analyzing every aspect of the road, shifting gears constantly. When one overthinks, they avoid confronting any unacceptable thought, situation, or behavior. They show no emotion, as they have distanced themselves from the unwanted thought or impulse with the analysis of it. For instance, a person may have been informed that he has a terminal illness. Rather than express the sadness that should be associated with this terrible news, they become involved in searching for impossible cures.

11) Rationalization – I like to compare this defense mechanism to "Sour Grapes." One tends to put a different light on an undesirable situation. You were dating a wonderful girl, and she drops you out of the blue. You take a step back and conclude that she really wasn't the right girl for you anyway.

12) Undoing – This defense mechanism pretty much defines itself. You want to take back a behavior or an insult that was harmful. You spend much time attempting to be overly pleasant to that individual, hoping that the golden treatment might balance out the harm done.

Mature Defense Mechanisms:

13) Sublimation – This defense mechanism channels unacceptable thoughts, emotions, or impulses into more acceptable ways of coping with life's struggles. Suppose you have some sexual impulses that you do not want to act upon. You pack up your gym bag and redirect that energy into some rigorous exercise. Sublimation can also be expressed in humor and fantasy. As far as I am concerned, humor is the

most mature of all defense mechanisms. It enables one to decrease the intensity of the situation with laughter. Fantasy can channel unattainable desires into imagining alternative career goals. Hey, I am sixty-one and never thought I would write a book, but I always wanted to. As a Baby Boomer, I am very much interested in helping my fellow boomers to join me in attaining a goal or dream set long ago and thought to be unattainable.

14) Compensation – This is a process where we attempt to counterbalance our weaknesses with our strengths. "I may not be able to _____ (you fill in the blank) but I sure can _____!" This method helps reinforce our self-esteem and our self- image.

15) Assertiveness – If we can all learn to emphasize our needs in a thoughtful and respective manner and direct those needs to the proper person, then we have developed one of the most desired coping skills. It is a very effective defense mechanism.

Were you able to identify any of the defense mechanisms above? I hope so. Once we know what gear we are in and make the proper adjustments, we can get into Drive and continue on our way.

The proper adjustments you ask? I am referring to some psychotherapy. These defense mechanisms aren't written in stone. Your gear is not stuck. Please know that! Through cognitive awareness and changes, we can begin to challenge the unhealthy ways we are coping and begin to substitute more mature ones.

What do they say? The journey begins but with a single step. Let's make our journey a peaceful one by beginning to get us into the proper gear.

Chapter 6

The Gas Pedal
or
"I Think I Can, I Think I Can."

In the previous chapters we examined some personalities and defense mechanisms that help to create our basic driving skills. Now, let's take a more in depth look at our coping skills.

Our hands may control the steering wheel, but our foot controls the gas pedal. How revved up are we in meeting today's challenges? Our miles per hour are similar to how we cope. So, I ask you, how capable are you in dealing with your stressors?

Some of us never know the answer to this question unless we are truly challenged. You know that saying; "Whatever doesn't kill us only makes us stronger"? There is some truth to that. Some individuals buckle under too much stress.

If coping mechanisms are like the gas pedal of the car, then giving it a little more gas should be effective in tackling that small hill.

Sometimes you just need a little more "energy" to get through the day. That energy just can't be retrieved from a bottle of "liquid boost" or whatever it is they advertise nowadays that will help "energize you." That so-called energy is your inner-strength, your ability to meet life's challenges.

All right. The hill becomes steeper. You apply more gas, and you complete the climb. Great! The car may have sputtered, but you hung in there, and you did it. Now the next time you face that hill, you might feel a sense of confidence that you can do this, again. I bet you never realized just how important that children's book, dealing with the Little Engine that could, really is. Confidence is a strong motivator in facing challenges. What is your confidence level?

Despite confidence and despite a well-equipped set of coping skills, there may be challenges that overwhelm us. Ever flood the car by applying too much gas? The car just won't turn on. The mechanic advises you to wait a few minutes and try again – with less pressure on that pedal. You need to try a different approach.

For those times that we do become unable to start-up – when we are over flooded with challenges that prevent us from even getting down our own driveways, please do not give up. The yellow light on our dashboard may have turned to red, but we can handle this.

If you watched old Woody Allen films, then you were introduced to therapy and the prime example of a very anxious person. Now, obviously one does not have to have his heightened anxiety state to seek help. But every now and then, some individuals need some supportive therapy – someone to talk to and to engage with. A therapist can help you develop or reinforce some healthy defense mechanisms.

Another form of therapy is referred to as CBT – Cognitive Behavioral Therapy. I have often discussed that our perceptions can influence the way we think, feel, and behave. You see, it is our thoughts, not the external events, people, or situations that control our feelings and behaviors. By changing the way we perceive or think about certain events, people, or situations, we can change the way we feel and the way we behave.

This is where Jerry's mantra always comes in handy. I have faced in my lifetime some very significant and life-changing challenges, and I am here to tell you that I have survived them. I have faith that you can, too.

I hope that having read this chapter, you will be more aware of your own coping mechanisms. You don't have to wait for that steep hill or unexpected turn in the road to seek help.

Mental Wellness is you deciding to take care of you! Sometimes a bubble bath will do. And one of these days, I do plan to have a body massage. But the most important aspect of taking care of yourself is managing the way you think, the way you feel, and the way you behave. It is a true gift to have a gas pedal that can respond to all of life's challenges.

The Gas Tank
or
"Don't Over Tap"

One of the psychiatric disorders most near and dear to my heart is substance abuse and dependence. Why? It is often never addressed in the primary care physician's office, yet it is the leading cause of deaths among teens.

As far as adults, a simple questionnaire consisting of only four questions can alert the clinician to any possible problem and takes less than a minute to administer. It is referred to as the CAGE questionnaire – one of many mnemonics I will be addressing in the book. This particular CAGE has been adopted to include drugs:

1. Have you felt you ought to cut down on your drinking or drug use?
2. Have people annoyed you by criticizing your drinking or drug use?
3. Have you felt bad or guilty about your drinking or drug use?
4. Have you ever had a drink or used drugs first thing in the morning to steady your nerves or to get rid of a hangover (eye-opener)?

Each positive response is given 1 point. A total of 2 points is considered clinically significant for substance abuse or dependence and requires further investigation.

One introductory question I use before I administer the CAGE is, "Do you feel that you have to use alcohol or drugs as a means of self-medicating?" This question is less threatening and they often are willing to admit that they will have a quick drink before giving a speech, or use alcohol as a means of making social situations less intimidating. Some moms will admit to taking a "shot" before the kids get off of the school bus. "A rough day at work can only be relieved by Scotch and soda or a Martini."

I think it is important to discuss the two different forms of problem drinking that I deal with in my profession. The term alcoholic can be very pejorative to some. It refers to alcohol dependence. These individuals show signs of physical addiction to alcohol, being able to tolerate increased quantities over time and can develop withdrawal signs if the body does not receive its usual dose. The other distinguishing factor is that despite problems in physical or mental health, or problems in family or social relationships and job responsibilities, they continue to drink. This indicates a loss of control of the substance. Their lives become dominated with obtaining that next drink. The same criteria can be applied to drugs as well.

Now, alcohol abuse can certainly lead to problems as well, but the distinguishing factor is the absence of physical addiction. In other words, little to no tolerance, no withdrawal but some incredible hangovers, and no problems with control issues. They have not crossed that delicate line where the substance begins to consume and control their lives. But it can happen at any time. So many alcohol abusers become cavalier in their drinking habits. One day they may sadly discover that the point of no return has been breached.

I had referred in a previous chapter to family histories. Although there tends to be a familial pattern, there is no known cause of alcohol abuse or dependence. Some individuals can drink in a very responsible manner and never deal with control issues. Others can cross the line into dependence much more readily.

Risk factors have been identified, in addition to having an immediate family member with the diagnosis. Peer pressure, especially teens and college students can place themselves at higher risk. Did you know that the risk of becoming an alcoholic if you are an alcohol abuser is ten to fifteen percent? However, the younger one begins to use alcohol, the higher the risk becomes. For instance, forty percent of teens who started drinking at age thirteen or younger developed alcohol dependence later in life. Waiting until age seventeen puts them more closely in the ten to fifteen percent category.

When you consider that motor vehicle accidents are the number one killer of our beautiful teenagers, then it is time to step in and decrease their likelihood of turning to drugs and alcohol. Is alcohol accessible to them in your home? Do you live in a community where there is a high social acceptance of alcohol use? How safe do you think your child is? Have you talked to them about their drug or alcohol use? If not, please do. It could save a life.

And of course, psychiatric conditions such as depression, bipolar disorder, anxiety disorders, or schizophrenia increase the rate of developing alcohol abuse and dependence. What happens when some of my clients become overwhelmed with stressors or feel that their meds are just too slow to respond? They may self-medicate which complicates their psychiatric conditions. Not only will they be compromising their health, preventing adequate response to their medications, but also their drinking can just cause them to throw caution to the wind and forget to take their medication.

If you are overfilling your gas tank, please assess why? I cannot force you to change your habits, nor can I force you to seek help. You need to want to make that difference in your life.

Please do the CAGE assessment honestly. Then, in keeping with mental wellness, get help before the yellow light turns to red. There are so many clinicians out there trained to deal with these issues. Promise me that you will seek help. Do it for yourself. Do it for your family.

Chapter 8

The Muffler and Exhaust
or
"Please Keep it Down, You Motor-mouth!"

Have we not all been guilty of "blowing off some steam" once in a while? We get angry, and sometimes we just blurt out our thoughts and fail to count to ten. And at other times we can manage to maintain some dignity and either remain silent or give appropriate feedback in a non-threatening manner. It is a challenge at times, but if you can avoid conflict and "muffle" yourself, then this chapter is not directed at you.

This chapter is devoted to those individuals that have anger-management issues. You know who you are. You have a low tolerance level towards others. People walk around you as if they are walking on eggshells.

Anger-management problems can be related to a number of psychiatric conditions. This chapter includes the diagnoses I see most often in my office.

Some personality disorders naturally display their anger. Borderlines often have swift reactivity to a situation, going from calm to ballistic in a matter of milliseconds. This inability to tolerate small stressors is related to their very poor capacity to cope with frustration. I am saddened to see the scars they bear on their forearms, as some of these individuals are cutters.

You might think that the anti-social personalities have anger management issues. On the contrary, they can be very engaging. But I would keep my distance. They have a Swiss cheese superego.

Obviously, bipolar disorder, previously known as manic-depressive disorder, has mood instability at the core of the illness. Irritability can be seen in the depressive state and in the mixed state especially. The mixed state is described as symptoms of anxiety and irritability experienced in addition to their depression. Unfortunately, the term bipolar is used often to describe someone who is moody, but does not necessarily meet the full criteria of the illness. However, someone who is observed having increased irritability, different from their normal observed state of interacting with others, could be a yellow warning light that further assessment is necessary.

Depression can also have irritability as a symptom. Seasonal affective changes can bring on irritability. And I discussed PMS in earlier chapters. Again, further diagnosis is needed.

I believe one the most educational rotations in my psychiatric residency was to work with Vietnam veterans. I was able to easily diagnosis PTSD or post-traumatic stress disorder in these individuals. One of the clusters of symptoms involves heightened body arousal. Anger management issues were one of the most frequently experienced symptoms in this cluster. Most complained that they were unable to keep a job as they had arguments with their bosses ending in dismissal.

And that complaint of the "inability to hold down a job" became a warning sign for me to dig deeper into the history of my non-veteran patients. Often times, young men and women would be forced to see me in community mental health settings with anger management issues. When asked about their childhood experiences, most of the individuals who experienced sexual or extreme physical abuse had symptoms similar or identical to PTSD. Anger management issues became a way of their dealing with the world. They were deprived of that whole important part of their childhood and the developmental milestones so necessary for healthy defense mechanisms to be incorporated into their psyche.

And finally, I deal with individuals who just have substance abuse issues. Alcohol and drugs can cause changes in one's ability to interact appropriately with others. Disinhibition occurs and behaviors, not normally seen when sober, rear their ugly heads.

Anger related to personality disorders can benefit from psychotherapy. The other disorders I mentions above, including bipolar disorder, depression, PTSD and substance abuse require further assessment and treatment, and often are prescribed medication to help manage their symptoms.

Muffler issues do not have to exist. Many individuals who are willing to acknowledge that they may have a problem being too loud too often, and are disturbing the people they interact with should make an appointment with a mental health professional.

Chapter 9

The Rearview Mirror
or
"I Can't Stop Looking Back"

I mentioned that rearview mirror, didn't I? Sometimes we look back much too often. Yes, our childhood may not have been perfect. I have met some unfortunate clients whose rearview mirror is so contaminated with abusive situations that it has widened to a point where it blocks their windshield. No matter how much windshield wiper fluid I attempt to pour into their reservoir, they can't move forward. Their perceptions and feelings prevent their foot from coming off the brake pedal.

Of course our past has helped create the person we are today – the way we interpret our environment and the way we react to it. It is when the past becomes the focus of our day that the yellow light appears.

I have mentioned the many developmental theorists who regard our childhood as playing a significant role in the assembly line of our psyche. The lack of nurturance, childhood abuse, and trauma can leave significant dents and scratches on the chassis, as well as flawing the inner circuitry. The rearview mirror can be terrorizing to these individuals. Either it completely blocks their ability to see the road ahead, or they avoid looking at it completely and end up being miserable drivers, affecting themselves and others. Many of these individuals have personality disorders or traits. PTSD and Depression are also results of trauma or inadequate coping.

And it is not just childhood events that can affect the rearview mirror. Many of my clients are affected by the economy and have real financial worries. They lay their heads on the pillow at night and ruminate about their plights.

I have also seen marriages that have lasted for years end in divorce. In many cases, it was not a mutual decision, and the wronged spouse and the grown children can be in a state of disbelief.

Individuals often come to my office with a concern that they might be depressed or that their anxiety has worsened. Most of these clients have no significant past history of a mental disorder so, of course, the emergence of these symptoms has brought them to my office. They recognized the yellow light. And in addition to no previous history of depression or anxiety, the symptoms seemed to appear within 3 months of a stressful life event. This signifies an Adjustment Disorder.

The death of a loved one can cause significant depression. The bereavement process has, unfortunately, been experienced by most of us. I liken it to the waves on the ocean. Initially, you are hit hard and steady as those hurricane sized waves come crashing down. As time goes by, the hurricane is reduced to a tropical storm, and the intense pain and energy of the wave is less likely to knock you off of your feet. Some individuals are soon able to lie on the beach and look out at the waves and again see the beauty in their swirls, their white foamed caps, the way they edge up to your toes. They respect the sand castle you have begun to recreate. Then, out of the blue, you hear a song – in my case, Izzy singing, "Somewhere Over the Rainbow" – and the waves become a little stronger. You accept the process, knowing that the sand castle may lose a bit of its fortress. You take a deep breath and begin to reinforce that castle's buttress. You lower the drawbridge. You clean out the moat. You look up to the heavens with a tear in your eye, and you blow a kiss to heaven.

There are some individuals who remain in that hurricane state. This is termed pathological grief. Of course the death of a loved one changes our lives forever. Some individuals allow this loss to consume them and to prevent them from ever taking another journey.

The purpose of the rearview mirror is to help us continue our journey ahead. If the yellow light is on, then we need to adjust that mirror.

I hope that anyone who is unable to again see the beauty in the waves or begin to reconstruct their sand castle, seek help for their condition. There is hope. I know this to be true.

Chapter 10

The Chassis
or
"Does My Back Bumper Look Too Wide to You?"

Before we talk about the journey and address all of the environmental stressors or influences that manage to lie on our path, I felt that it was important to discuss another topic that may influence the way we feel about ourselves. Remember – the way we feel about ourselves can influence our behavior.

As always, I have no shame in using myself as an example. After all, if I can't look at myself honestly, how can I expect others to do so?

When I was doing my radiology residency, my call started at 5 P.M. and was primarily devoted to reading all of the ER films. Since I was associated with a very large Cleveland hospital, I never found time to break away for a nutritious dinner. And did I ever prepare for this by packing a few items in a lunch pail? No! Life was too hectic. I had three children in grade school and a busy husband who was out the door before 7 A.M. so that he could get home to feed the family and see homework assignments were done. Thanks, Jim. I don't think you realize how much I appreciated you back then.

Anyway, the vending machine room (and I emphasize room because there was every snack available) was adjacent to the X-ray reading room. Well, all I had to do was to make sure I packed plenty of one-dollar bills to get me through the night. And of course my sensitive reward center in my brain just loved that chocolate bar and craved another. As a result, I was loading on twenty pounds a year. Because I wore scrubs, I never really noticed the gradual increments, but as the years progressed, I was not the lovely, slender woman that started residency. And during the fourth year (are you all doing the math?), I was blimpy. I felt terrible about myself. What was interesting is that I never noticed much of a change when I looked in the sink mirror to apply makeup. But, my God, if someone took a picture of me, I stared at this stranger in utter disbelief. That can't be me. The photo must have been shot with a wide-angle lens. Afraid not, Elaine. You are fat. And guess what? Other people noticed it, too. As a matter of fact, I noticed a significant change in others' behavior toward me. Some of my male attendings that were very respectful initially were now treating me differently. Not all, just some.

I recall watching a show on TV where a model was fitted with a fat suit and walked the streets of New York to educate herself on the discrimination towards obese individuals.

I am white and experienced very little discrimination in my lifetime. The only other episode was from my organic chemistry professor at Case. I went back to school at age thirty-eight to prove to the med school dean that cobwebs were not forming and that I was an excellent candidate for the class of '89. He requested that I enroll in some classes such as organic chemistry and biochemistry. I walked into a class of at least 200 brilliant looking students and made sure I sat at the back. I stood out like a sore thumb. But you know what, I loved that class. And when I ran home like a kid with the highest score in the class after the first exam, my husband said, "I think you can handle med school. It's a go as far as I am concerned."

During the remainder of that semester, I was neck and neck with a young Asian student, setting the curve for the class. As a result, my professor asked me to meet with him in his office one day. He actually said, "I don't get it. Why are you scoring so high?" I looked at him and said matter-of-factly, "Because I am that smart." He had seen an older woman in his class and drew unfounded conclusions. I asked him if he thought I was cheating. He reassured me that he did not but just called me an enigma. Well! Call me what you want, I am who I am. And the happy ending to this story is that I entered med school in 1989 and can describe those next four years as some of the best years of my life – thanks to a supportive husband and three children who sometimes joined me for lectures.

We all have faced discrimination. I will never begin to compare my small encounters with those faced by others with different colors of skin, with different religions, or with different life styles. Discrimination runs a wide gamete. If you are not a certain height or dress size, you are ostracized from being a model. If your facial features aren't perfect you may be judged.

Imagine, people thinking that they know us just by looking at our chassis. They never bothered stepping inside the car, getting to know the driver.

There was a story told to me long ago so I have forgotten the details. But it revolved around a father sitting in a subway with three young children who were running around the car, upsetting other passengers. The father seemed to be unfazed by their excitement and sat, just staring into space. A very annoyed passenger finally scolded him. He looked up, tears in his eyes, and offered a big apology. He had explained that they were returning from the hospital where his young wife had died of breast cancer, and that his children, too young to comprehend, were experiencing some joy in their play, and that he was allowing them this little time of excitement before the whole world of funeral planning and news of the loss of their mother came crashing down when they reached home. The whole demeanor of the passengers changed from anger to compassion. Knowledge is a powerful thing!

There is another saying I am sure you are all aware of. Please do not assume. It makes an ass of "u" and me.

So, a chassis can influence how we feel and how we behave. I have the privilege of working in an office that offers not only the ability to mentally think positively of yourself, but also the ability to physically think positively of yourself.

I have always wanted to age gracefully. And I still plan to do so. But define gracefully? I will confess that if I have a bump here or a dent there, I just may have it removed. Does that make me less respectable as a person? That I gave in to vanity? Of course not. I know what my self-esteem runs on. I could have wrinkles galore and put back those 80 pounds and still not change inside. My mantra of what other people think, say, or do has strengthened me. I don't need to be perfect to feel good about myself. But sometimes, doing something special for me is a good thing. If I am doing it because of a poor self-esteem, then I am defeating the purpose. You have to change your inside first. A strong engine and resilient driving attitude can drive into the body shop at any time. Please don't think it works the other way around.

Remember the saying, "A leopard can't change its spots"? Well the leopard depends on its natural instincts. We are different. We can change our perceptions, our feelings and our behavior. That is what I have been stressing all along. If you want to change your spots, your self-esteem is intact, and you are doing it for the rights reasons, then you certainly have my blessing.

By the way, my back fender is less wide, thank heavens, but now lacks form. Gravity took over. But that's OK. And my boobies are not 40 D anymore but 40 long with the right a little longer than the left. I have extra flesh on my abdomen where the vending machines had once taken over. Who knows? I may drive this baby into a body shop one day. After all, as Robert Frost had written, "I have promises to keep and miles to go before I sleep, and miles to go before I sleep."

Chapter 11

The Classic Car
or
A Chapter Devoted to Baby Boomers

I started a blog last summer entitled "WE ARE BOOMING." I decided to put a passage from my blog into this book. Since my generation seemed to be somewhat challenged at computers and new-aged ways of communicating, such as blogging, I never got many hits. So I have not kept up with it.

I turned my energies to writing this book on mental wellness. After all, one of the first blogs I wrote was devoted to "No Regrets," and I always wanted to write this book. I had written children's books before but never published them. Tummy Town was written for my children to teach them about better nutrition. It has delightful characters such as Betsy Burger, Barney Bun, Anna Banana, and the Frenchy Fry Can-Can Dancers who were kicked out of the nightclub because they got the dance floor all greasy. The Hot Potato Juggler was brought in as a substitute. Feelingdale was the home of Shy Violet, I.C. Green, Tickled Pink, and the town bully, Ira Red along with other interesting characters. Well, people in the town learned that talking about their feelings was a good thing. It also talked about the town bully and how to better deal with him.

So here I am, trying to set an example for my fellow baby boomers. I decided to have "no regrets." The passage also explains why I wanted to focus attention to this important age group. After all, the oldest members will turn sixty-five this year (2011). They may retire but not have planned fully for it. They may be faced with caring for older parents. Younger members of the age group may be new empty nesters, facing different challenges, such as loneliness or keeping the marriage fresh.

Whatever the challenge, I do not want any of us to give up on our dreams. So here is an excerpt from my first attempt at blogging.

NO REGRETS

Hello to all of my wonderful Baby Boomers,

I know you are out there. But blogging was not in our vocabulary growing up - nor was twitting, nor YouTube, nor Facebook. My daughter signed me up for the new age way of communicating (note daughter signed me up as I couldn't get it), but I still don't use it properly. I have several friends and family on Facebook and actually send them my posting every Sunday. My sister Eloise hoots and toots on in, and she is only eighteen months younger than I am. How can I reach a generation that doesn't use this form of communication?

You know this whole Baby Boomer obsession of mine was born from an idea for a talk show. Oprah had offered this opportunity to anyone who had a dream of hosting his or her own show. I will be honest - that was not my dream at the time. But I submitted a video that voiced my concerns about my generation. The more I listened to my own words, the more I appreciated the need to continue my quest. I was not selected, obviously, but now it has become a dream, a passion. TV shows are what many of my generation are quite comfortable with. I could have reached so many more boomers had I been selected to compete. So what did I do? I decided to blog my thoughts, my concerns. Thus, We Are Booming was created. Not the best means of communicating, but it will do for now. I would have regretted not following through with the desire to talk to my generation. And if a handful are able to enjoy it - YEAH! It's a handful of folks I never reached before.

One of my regrets in the video was the lack of emphasis on

the "No Regrets" segment of that talk show. Here we are between the ages of 46 and 64 turning 65. Who does that include? New empty nesters? Grandparents? If you are fortunate to have a job, you may be facing retirement this year. You may be overwhelmed with stressors and be required to dig down deep to cope with things that you never thought would happen - loss of a job, a failed marriage. I have a dear friend whose divorce was just finalized after thirty years of marriage. Sad, but true. But today's posting is not to address the stressors or the current state we find ourselves in. It is to ask you to go to that place inside - maybe deep in your heart or in the private recesses of your beautiful mind and ask yourself, "What would make me happy today? " Or, "What did I want to do that I never got a chance to do?" I want you to put your needs first. This may not feel natural. And may I stress that this isn't being selfish. Don't you ever think that for a moment. Remember the stewardess always warning us to put our oxygen masks on first before placing it on our child? Did you ever think to yourself, "Absolutely not. My child's safety matters the most!" Of course we think that way but the important lesson is that, unless you are OK, no one else will be.

Well - I am asking all of you to do something for yourselves. It could be something so simple as to connect with an old friend or family member. May I suggest Facebook (that is if you have someone around to help)? You may have envisioned yourself in better shape at this age. No regrets mind you. Look in the mirror, appreciate your inner beauty, and set out to tweak yourself. I joined Weight Watchers, and I bought these new age sneakers that promised to tone as I walked. I set out yesterday with my St. Bernard, Sampson. Unfortunately, his idea of walking was a slow lumber and our mile walk ended up in my worrying all afternoon over his panting and recovery from such exercise. Want to take a trip?

Mine would be to visit Italy where I could feast upon the art and the pasta. I received a Rosetta Stone Italian set from Santa. I am taking baby steps towards a few goals.

I have no regrets when it comes to my spirituality. God has become so important in my life. Letting go and letting God has been a lifesaver for me. Certain events have happened in my life recently that I believe He has had a hand in. I had the good fortune to reconnect with my med school colleague, Dr. David Parajon, who, along with his wife Dr. Laura, reside in Nicaragua and meet the needs of so many less fortunate. So, I have added a larger goal to my life - to actually be a medical missionary to Nicaragua. I hope to set aside two weeks a year to visit them and do what is necessary to help.

What are your dreams? What is standing in your way? Life is too short, my friends, to not take a chance. Call up your local community college for a brochure. Take a walk. Put daisies on your table. Enjoy the simplicities and make your day a better one.

I have the privilege of calling Gai Russo a friend. Just being with her elevates me to a better place. She makes the air I breathe sweeter. Her kind soul is reflected in her eyes. She also happens to be a brilliant jewelry designer.

She has been very supportive of me throughout the years. After my son, Andy, died, she made Peace jewelry as she knew that that was his favorite thing to say, "Peace." The other day I received a package in the mail. She sent me a "NO REGRETS" bracelet. I will never take it off, Gai. Thank you for believing in me and my dreams.

And I plan to finish a book on Mental Wellness and rekindle my children's books. "No regrets" has become a part of me.

So, my dear Baby Boomers, what are you plans for today? Are you looking ahead to the holidays? Are you hoping to accomplish something this month? This year? Please let me hear from you. I am sending you "NO REGRETS" karma through my blog.

Love and Peace to you all. Dr. Elaine

So there it is. And I am glad I included it. Doing something positive for ourselves is necessary for Mental Wellness. And as we learned in the defense mechanism chapter, sublimation is a very health defense mechanism. It can be expressed through humor or fantasy.

What is your fantasy? What is a goal you never accomplished? Write it down, and make it part of your journey.

Chapter 12

Snow Tires
or
"Not Another Cleveland Winter!"

I am writing this book in the dead of winter. As a Clevelander, the meteorological effects of Lake Erie affect our winters. We can have some pretty nasty snowfalls, temperature drops, and wind chill factors. As a result, we have a very sophisticated way of alerting parents of school closings.

And yet, Cleveland is blessed with incredible Metro Parks. My home in Moreland Hills is nestled up against huge pine trees that catch the snowflakes and morning light so beautifully. I see new deer tracks every time I take my St. Bernard, Sampson, for a walk. They have become shortened walks, but walks nonetheless. He always detects that deer were previously prancing through the yard and throws a bass-toned bark in their direction just in case the deer were not aware that this is his property. I hear wild turkeys in the morning and have seen black squirrels scurry around the trees. I live in a winter wonderland. This picture postcard setting takes my breath away.

So, I guess what I am driving at is there are a few ways of looking at winter. Let's look at the negative aspects of winter.

Winter weather can contribute to road hazards and motor vehicle accidents. We have discussed the effects that trauma can have on individuals. I have diagnosed PTSD among those clients who have encountered MVA's and are unable to get behind the steering wheel again.

And then there are the shorter days of winter. Many individuals begin to feel somewhat melancholic when the sun sets before dinner is served. These seasonal affective changes are very interesting to me not only from a psychiatric perspective, but also a physiological one.

Why do animals instinctually know how to survive the long winter? Well, bears and other hibernators begin to manufacture increased amounts of melatonin. You see, sunlight, hitting the back of our eye, or retina, inhibits production of melatonin in a beautifully designed biochemical process that I won't bore you with here. As the length of sunlight is shortened, production of melatonin is increased. Bears react to increased melatonin by going nighty-night.

Now, could this lack of sunlight also affect humans? Actually, despite Seasonal Affective Disorder not being recognized as a specific disorder, it is a "specifier" for depressive disorder. My clients enjoy life to its fullest in warm months, but come late fall to early spring, they become mildly depressed, year after year. Many use Light Boxes, designed to simulate sunlight and trick the eye into believing it is July. This therapy does not consistently work for all of these individuals, but it is an alternative to those opposed to taking medication during these few months.

So, how do we prepare for winter? I have a 4-wheel drive vehicle. My husband needs to have snow tires to navigate the slightest of inclines. Others do Hail Mary's as they turn out of their driveways.

In this chapter, I addressed two concerns I have for winter weather. It can cause more accidents, and it can cause the onset of depressive symptoms.

I hope that the yellow warning light of winter's effects encourages you to seek help for symptoms. There are treatment options that are available to you.

The other point I was attempting to make is to look for the beauty in your surroundings. Try to make lemonade out of lemons. Well, if we are talking about winter I should be referring to hot cocoa but you know what I mean.

Speaking of lemons, let me just add here that none of us are defective. There may be a lemon law in your state that applies to your automobile, but as far as the human spirit, there is good in every one of us. If you are convinced that you are flawed, I hope this book begins to challenge that thought.

Positive thinking not only affects the mind, but the body as well. I had a very wonderful friend that I was privileged to know and to curl with. (You know – that funny game on ice). She was undergoing radiation therapy and chemotherapy for advanced ovarian cancer. She was terminal and was given a brief period to live. But evidently she refuted that prognosis. She was the first person to discuss making lemonade with me. Being an artist, she would paint smiley faces or colorful balloons on her abdomen near the site of her radiation markers. She wanted to cheer up the staff that worked in oncology. She was always thinking of others and not herself. When they unwrapped her dressings, they were greeted with her beautiful artwork, which reflected her attitude. She always brought a smile to their faces. It matched her beautiful smile. She never complained about her fate, would never complain about her pain or weakness, and lived each day to its fullest. She lived much longer than expected. She was not running on fumes as the medical community thought. She was running on her inner strength. Never underestimate its power.

Chapter 13

Wheel Alignment
or
"What Do You Mean I'm Unstable?"

Ever sense that your wheels are out of alignment? Isn't there some type of stabilizing contraption to accommodate the uneven road? A small bump can cause your head to miss the top of the car by millimeters if everything is out of sorts. You are up and down; up and down.

This is how clients describe their moods to me. They know all of the terminology. "Doc, I am such a rapid-cycler." "My moods are completely unstable."

Well, bipolar disorder can certainly be the underlying cause. However, there are other explanations for poor mood control that I have referred to in previous chapters.

In addition to bipolar disorder, depression and anxiety can cause irritability that can appear as moodiness.

Certain personality disorders are prone to show mood reactivity. And PTSD can also lead to anger management issues.

Chapter 17 deals with criteria for bipolar illness, as well as other disorders. If, however, you are diagnosed with bipolar disorder and your moods are unstable, just as the alignment of your car, then certain medications called mood stabilizers are very helpful in bringing you back into balance.

That reminds me again of the stigma of mental illness. So many of my clients who are bipolar refer to their condition as a "chemical imbalance of the brain." Are they really wrong? We have closely examined some of the neurotransmitters that can be out of balance and produce symptoms such as depression, anxiety, and hypomania or mania.

A medication I often prescribe to my bipolar patients is termed a mood-stabilizer. Interestingly, most mood stabilizers are anti-epileptic medication such as Depakote, Lamictal, Trileptal, Tegretol, Keppra, and Topamax, to name a few. How do these medications stabilize moods? To be honest, I am not aware of the exact mechanism, but I often suspected that a medication that can quiet the brain to prevent seizures might also be capable of keeping it a bit more stabilized.

Newer atypical anti-psychotics are also showing promise in stabilizing mood swings. Geodon, Seroquel, and Abilify are to name a few.

Whatever the diagnosis, mood swings can interfere with function and require further treatment.

Please don't wait too long when the yellow light appears. Untreated bipolar symptoms can impact the prognosis and prolong the response to treatment.

Chapter 14

Luxurious Options
or
"What Do You Mean Your Steering Wheel is Heated?"

The purpose of this chapter is to emphasize the fact that mental illnesses do not discriminate. They can affect the young and the old, men, women, and children regardless of gender, race, ethnicity, and socio-economic status. You could be driving the most luxurious car, or your car could be on cinder blocks in the background. Your car affords you no immunity.

According to the World Health Organization, one in every four people will develop one or more mental disorders at some stage in their life.

I have stressed all along in this book that treatment works. Yet, as many as two-thirds of individuals with a diagnosable mental disorder do not seek treatment. I have suggested possible reasons – the stigma of mental illness, the fear that the treatment may be worse than the illness itself, the lack of awareness, and the lack of access and affordability of care.

Wouldn't it be wonderful to approach mental illness through preventative means and reduce such staggering statistics? After all, mental illnesses are more common than cancer, diabetes, or heart disease and rank first among illnesses that cause disability in the United States, Canada, and Western Europe.

Mental Wellness is a very noble cause, don't you agree? By recognizing early warning signs and seeking treatment in a timely fashion, we could reduce these staggering statistics. It certainly is worth a try.

Chapter 15

Suicide
or
"The Car Remains in the Garage"

This is a very difficult topic to introduce in such a light-hearted book. As I mentioned in the preface, I have lost patients to this fatal decision of theirs to end the pain and suffering.

And that is exactly what it is. Individuals who are so overwhelmed with stress, with pain, with exhausted coping mechanisms, or clearly, ineffective ones, and a lack of a support system see suicide as their only means of turning off the mental anguish. And if they happened to use any alcohol or drugs to self-medicate, then their inhibitions and their better judgment are compromised, and the risk of their attempting or completing suicide has now increased.

Perhaps you are feeling so depressed and hopeless that, as you sit in the car, you find that you are no longer able to drive the car out of the garage. You contemplate whether or not to just shut the garage door and end it all.

Some people make those comments in my office, often very casually. They then look at my very concerned face and go on to convince me that it was just a thought – that they had no plan or intent. For, you see, I can sign a form, which happens to be pink in the state of Ohio, and hospitalize anyone whom I feel is a suicide threat to themselves. And since my patients know that and do not want to be "pink-slipped" they have to go through some intense assessment of their risk factors before they are permitted to leave my office. And let me emphasize here that despite many family members and friends viewing the individual's behavior as just attention-seeking and not a "cry for help," please think again. Every suicidal thought should always be taken seriously and further assessment is definitely required.

The reason I interrogate them so intently? Seventy-five percent of patients who do commit suicide demonstrated warning signs. I will list the warning signs and risks factors later in this chapter. But first I want to share some other concerning data.

I am a very proud Baby Boomer. The oldest of our group will turn sixty-five this year. In June 2010, the New York Times reported that for the second year in a row, baby boomers had suffered the highest rate of suicide in the United States. Prior to this, those eighty years of age and older were most likely to take their own lives.

Another sad statistic is that at least fifty percent of the elderly had been to visit their doctor, not necessarily their psychiatrist, within the month of their suicide.

I can list all of the warning signs and risk factors to educate us all. However, there is one statistic that frightens me the most. Twenty five percent of completed suicides never gave a warning sign.

I have a story to share. When I first began training in the field of psychiatry, I was a nurse. I never planned to enter that field, but the night before I was to start my Public Health rotation, I broke my foot while jumping rope. Since I was unable to drive with a cast on my right foot and my apartment was just a two-minute walk (with crutches – three minutes) to the hospital, I was transferred to Psychiatry. And just let me take a moment to thank God for that life changing injury. My path started in psychiatry because of a spiral fracture to my fifth metatarsal. I am eternally grateful for my clumsiness.

There was a young, beautiful, and talented female patient on the ward who was severely depressed. I mentioned talented because she would sit at the piano in the patient lounge and play Chopin like I never heard it interpreted before. There was such emotion transposed from her fingers to the keyboard that her state of pain echoed off the corridor walls.

Back in the '70's there was no pressure to discharge the patient ASAP to release a bed to the intake department. We were able to monitor the ability of the patient to tolerate "off-ward" privileges. It would progress from walks with staff one-on-one, to walk with staff in a group. Then, when the patient was nearing discharge, we granted walks alone.

This lovely patient was restricted to the ward as her depression was so severe. Obviously, she had been admitted for suicidal thoughts and had previous admissions for missed suicide attempts. This history of past suicide attempts places her as a high-risk patient. Unfortunately, some of these patients are also dubbed "attention-seekers" by family or "frequent-flyers" by medical staff.

One morning, she enters the dining hall with a smile. She began to talk to staff and patients, stating that she was feeling one hundred percent better and was hoping to join the group walk that afternoon.

The staff interpreted her abrupt mood change as improvement. Her past history of missed suicide attempts must have been "you know, attention-seeking." So, not only was ward restriction lifted, but also walks one-on-one with staff. Her physician advanced her to the privilege of walks with staff and group. The group departed after lunch.

Minutes later, the staff and the group, minus our patient, returned to the ward. Police were notified of the missing female.

About thirty minutes later, we were informed that she had jumped off a building to her death just blocks away from the hospital.

I tell this story because I have never found this "very telling sign" of impending suicide listed on warnings or risk factors. Anyone who shows a sudden change in his or her mood, especially from depressed to happy and content within twenty-four hours is extremely suicidal. Why? They finally made up their mind to do it. The weight of the world is lifted off of their shoulders. Anyone who intends to complete the act will usually not tell anyone. If they want to die, they will die without any interference from others.

I have treated family members who have suffered from the loss of a loved one to suicide. One wife discovered her husband hanging in their garage. She was clueless regarding his intentions. Her PTSD is very severe as you can imagine.

Here are more statistics. One million people die of suicide worldwide. That is one death every forty seconds. In the United States, it is the eleventh leading cause of death. Every day, ninety-one people die of suicide in the United States. That is, one death every sixteen minutes.

If you consider that there are eleven to twenty-five attempts for every one completed suicide, then, of the 33,000 suicides listed in one year, there were 825,000 attempts.

It is the seventh leading cause of death in men and the sixteenth leading cause of death in women. Don't let that statistic fool you. Women lead men 2:1 in suicide attempts. However, men use more lethal means to commit suicide such as firearms and hangings where women are more likely to overdose.

Of the successful suicides, ninety percent had a mental disorder such as depression or substance abuse. I mentioned earlier the disinhibiting effects of alcohol and drugs. Well, one-third of victims tested positive for alcohol or drugs.

I want to list the warning signs for suicide. You will notice that many of these signs or symptoms will appear in future chapters listing the specific criteria for depression and bipolar disorder.

Warning signs include:
Abrupt changes in personality
Giving away possessions

Previous suicide attempt

Use of drugs and/or alcohol

Change in eating pattern - *significant weight change*

Change in sleeping pattern - *insomnia/oversleeping*

Unwillingness or inability to communicate

Depression

Extreme or extended boredom

Accident prone (carelessness)

Unusual sadness, discouragement, and loneliness

Talk of wanting to die

Neglect of academic work and/or personal appearance

Family disruptions - divorce, trauma, losing loved one

Running away from home or truancy from school

Rebelliousness - reckless behavior

Withdrawal from people/activities they love

Confusion - Inability to concentrate

Chronic Pain, Panic, or Anxiety

Perfectionism

Restlessness

Risk factors include:

Problems with school or the law

Breakup of a romance

Unexpected pregnancy

A stressful family life (having parents who are depressed or are substance abusers, or a family history of suicide)

Loss of security (fear of authority, peers, group or gang members)

Stress due to new situations; college or relocating to a new community

Failing in school or failing to pass an important test

A serious illness or injury to oneself

Seriously injuring another person or causing another person's death (example: automobile accident)

Suffering a major loss (death of a loved one, loss of a home, divorce in the family, a sudden trauma, an ended relationship)

A sudden change in mood indicating that the depression had miraculously lifted

Although the above warning signs are important, please include the risk factors when assessing a loved one or friend. Combining the two lists will give you a more accurate profile of their suicide risk.

Before I leave this chapter, I want to provide you with a few resources should you have any concerns regarding yourself or a loved one.

My husband and I were very fortunate to meet Clark Flatt. He was the father of Jason, a beautiful 16 year old, who committed suicide on July 16, 1997. Clark established Jason's Foundation, devoted to the silent epidemic of youth suicide. I urge you to contact this foundation if you are concerned about a teenaged family member or friend. Their website is www.jasonfoundation.com.

If for any reason you or your family member is involved in a crisis, please dial 911.

Sometimes, you just need to reach out and talk to someone. The suicide hotline is:

1-800-SUICIDE or 1-800-784-2433.

Chapter 16

Your Dashboard – The Diagnostic Exam
or
"Is a Yellow Light OK, or Can I Just Wait for the Red One?"

We may not have the luxury of car owners to be given a yellow warning light indicating that something needs to be serviced. And certainly the color change to a vibrant red might as well have an audio attached saying, "Hey dummy, how long were you planning to press your luck? Your mechanic bill just quadrupled in cost."

Let's face it. As human beings, we have a number of reasons to ignore the yellow warning lights. The fear that something might actually be wrong is the most difficult to overcome. Complete denial that the car is fine and it must be a short in the electrical system is another popular misconception. You can't afford to follow-up with the mechanic due to money or insurance issues have become a sign of the times. Or you just might be one of those risk takers that enjoys living on the edge.

Well, I can tell you that all of these thought processes, if you will, can interfere with your seeking help. Don't you really just want to turn off that damned yellow light? And the excuses? I have heard them all. If I am lucky enough to have someone present me with concerns about their light problem, we could avoid the breakdown at the side of the road just waiting to happen. The red light issues often present in crisis and require much more intense workups, including a possible need for hospitalization. Who wants that?

And I must admit that there are a few in my practice that are completely stabilized from symptoms that first led them to my office. Now they come in for maintenance checkups. A smooth running engine without any significant symptoms is a wonderful motivator for continuing to feel that way. I love doing maintenance checkups and so do my clients.

So how do I begin to convince drivers to pay attention to the yellow light? Yes, the yellow lights. My goal is to equip everyone with the knowledge of his or her dashboard and to intervene when necessary. A simple tune-up to identify the source behind that yellow light would be a good first step to mental wellness.

This is where I veer away from the levity of the yellow light. We have been talking about the symptoms that can cause them to appear. The point I am making is this: You know yourself better than anyone. I bet you could describe your personality or your normal modus operandi. So, when you don't "feel yourself," do you take the time to try to figure it out? Remember, there are a lot of influencing factors that can cause these changes. The change could be caused by, what I often refer to as "no-brainers" – loss of a job, marital or family problems, financial changes, death of a loved one, or a change in your health status. These social stressors obviously cause a change in your feelings, your moods, and your behaviors.

But what about that yellow light appearing without any significant precipitants? Are you perplexed and curious enough to pay attention to the changes you feel?

Ever think you have a handle on what is going on? Ever diagnose yourself? Believe me, I have bestowed the title of MD to some of my clients who feel that they know what is going on, demand what medication would be necessary because they saw the commercial on TV, or just read an article in a journal that absolutely clinches their problem. Believe me, I wish it were that simple. But it isn't.

Because my office does not contain the car mechanic's contraption, I am forced to rely on a good history of present symptoms, a chronological history of past psychiatric symptoms or diagnoses; investigating current ways of coping, knowing family history, and knowing their own medical history; examining their substance use; knowing what meds they are on, including over-the-counter and herbal meds; knowing their current stressors; and finding out whether any of the above information has led to a decline in function, whether in relationships or at their job. Sometimes, obtaining this amount of information from someone who is meeting me for the first time can be rather difficult. A primary goal I always plan in my first meeting, besides gathering all of the above information, is attempting to form a therapeutic alliance with my clients. It takes skill, compassion, and an excellent ear for hearing what the patient is really saying. It may be hidden, and it may take time and effort to put yourself in their situation, but if I can accomplish this, I will serve them well.

So you are hesitant to go through the above rig-a-ma-roll. Can't say I blame you, especially if you detect no yellow lights but do feel a mild change from normal functioning that may be causing a pale yellow to flicker.

So how do I begin to convince drivers to pay attentions to even a pale yellow light? Yes, even to that mild flicker. My goal is to equip everyone with the knowledge of his or her dashboard and to intervene when necessary. A simple tune-up to identify the source behind that yellow light would be a good first step to mental wellness.

Remember, there are a lot of influencing factors that can cause the yellow light to appear. Besides describing your symptoms, how you feel you cope on a day-to-day basis and the litany of current stressors you are facing, the family history is an essential part of the initial assessment.

Psychiatric conditions, such as depression, bipolar disorder, anxiety, schizophrenia, and substance abuse, follow a familial pattern; so a good family history is an essential part of the initial exam, as well. There is no guarantee that you would develop a certain disorder just because Dad or Aunt Martha has been diagnosed with it. But given certain circumstances, whether inadequate development of coping mechanisms, abuse of your body in a number of ways, or facing overwhelming stressors, the biological makeup of the brain can become altered, and certain symptoms may develop over time.

Let me give you an example. Substance abuse is much more common than you may think. If there is a history of alcoholism or drug abuse in your family, how have you been affected? Individuals who abuse alcohol – drink too much but can control consumption, upset others, and self-medicate for a number of reasons –can at some point in time cause a change in their brain's chemistry. They become addictive to the substance. They no longer can control their intake, they develop a tolerance to the substance, and they can manifest withdrawal symptoms specific to that substance.

So, our biological engine and chassis can be affected by a number of psychological and social factors. We will examine them more closely as we proceed to inspect our car.

Let me end this chapter by emphasizing that no matter what genetic or biological factors were thrown our way, the key to understanding ourselves is the knowledge of how our psychological makeup and our life's history have made us unique, not only in our appearance, but also in our thoughts, feelings and behaviors. In fact, this book will allow our vehicles to be geared up to take on the most difficult of journeys. You see knowledge is a powerful thing.

Chapter 17

The Diagnostic Assessment
or
"Plug Me in for the Answer to My Problem."

In the previous chapters, we have been discussing signs and symptoms. Just as the temperature gauge reads hot, and you roll into your mechanic's – or treat it yourself with coolant – so should you pay attention to the signs and symptoms you experience on your inner dashboard. You roll in to see me or another health inspector.

What a wonderful thing to have you in my office. I just obtained a wonderful history of your chief concerns, history of your present signs and symptoms, became aware of past medical and psychiatric history, reviewed your current meds, examined your substance abuse habits, questioned whether past abuse was in your history, assured myself that you were not homicidal or suicidal, and then began to proceed with the mental status exam.

I assessed your appearance and attitude. I noted the appropriateness of your behavior. I assessed your mood and effect, as well as anxiety level. I noted your speech. Your thought process was carefully analyzed for any loose associations or disorganization often seen in more serious conditions. Your thought content was examined for any delusional thoughts. And of course, I would get a laugh or a denial if I ask you if you were hearing or seeing things. Despite clients frequently denying this, I have my ways of determining if indeed you are hallucinating. Insight and judgment are evaluated. Often, I administer a mini-mental status exam to better assess memory, ability to abstract, detect flaws in orientation and reasoning, and to rule out dementia.

I now take all of this precious data and "plug you in." The purpose is to make a proper diagnosis.

Now, there are certain mnemonics in medicine that are helpful in reviewing symptoms and possibly pinpointing a diagnosis. Boy, there was one I learned in medical school for the cranial nerves that was similar to that dinghy, "There once was a man from Nantucket." Written by a man, I am sure. But there are some very useful mnemonics that can help confirm or rule out a diagnosis.

Here is one I use for depression: SIGECAPS.

S – Are you feeling sad, like your spark plugs and battery have been altered?

S – How are you sleeping? Too much? Too little? Feel like nodding at the wheel?

I – Have you been able to maintain your interests? Still taking those car trips?

G – Any problems with guilt, self-esteem, or self-worth? Avoiding the car mirror?

E – How is your energy? Are you running on empty?

C – How is your concentration? Paying attention to road signs? Missing turn-offs?

A – How is your appetite? Fuel tank filled? Oil checked lately?

P – Have passengers commented on psychomotor changes they see in your driving?

S – Have you had suicidal thoughts, plan or intent to drive the damn car off a cliff?

S – Have you found that the only way to make the journey is to keep a special bottle of fuel (substance) right next to you?

If you have been feeling sad or have experienced loss of pleasure or interest (anhedonia) and experience at least four of the other above symptoms for at least two weeks, you are depressed, my friend. I would encourage you to discuss these symptoms with your family doctor or with a psychiatrist. And if ever, ever you develop suicidal thoughts, I want you to go directly to the nearest emergency room for a suicide risk assessment.

Do you think you can motivate yourself to seek help should the yellow light of depression appear on your dashboard? I hope so. And please know that depression brings with it such negative thinking that would actually sabotage your getting treatment. You need to fight the urge to lie in bed and to ignore your symptoms.

I have a favorite poem that I often refer to when the going gets tough. It was written by a young man named William Ernest Henley who was afflicted with tuberculosis of the bone at age four. At age twenty-five, it had infected his foot, causing it to be amputated. At age twenty-six, he wrote the most inspiring poem I have every read. It was written from his hospital bed. It is entitled *Invictus,* meaning "undefeated" in Latin. He lived an active life until his death at age 53.

Invictus
Out of the night that covers me,
Black as the pit from pole to pole,
I thank whatever gods may be
For my unconquerable soul.
In the fell clutch of circumstance,
I have not winced nor cried aloud.
Under the bludgeoning of chance,
My head is bloody, but unbowed.
Beyond this place of wrath and tears
Looms but the Horror of the shade.
And yet the menace of the years
Finds and shall find me unafraid.
It matters not how strait the gate,
How charged with punishments the scroll.
I am the master of my fate.
I am the captain of my soul.

The biological distress the TB had caused and the sociological impact of having a foot amputated were no match for William Henley's psychological fortitude. He was the master of his fate, the captain of his soul. No yellow light, or should I say glaring red light, caused him to pull to the side of the road. He took the wheel of his car, and he enjoyed life's pleasures. He is my hero. I hope that he serves as a source of inspiration for you, too.

Stepping away from doom and gloom, I can guarantee that there are several yellow lights that can mean quite the opposite.

I am going to throw another mnemonic at you. I use it to diagnosis bipolar disorder: DIGFAST.

D – Are you easily distracted and easily frustrated? Have you flipped the bird today?

I – Are you an irresponsible driver or have erratic uninhibited behaviors?

G – Are you grandiose, feeling you have the right of way and own the road?

F – Do you have flight of ideas, paying less attention to the road?

A – Have you noticed more road trips and activities or passes through the ATM lane?

S – Are you sleeping less? Maybe you are out in the garage washing your car at 3 A.M.

T – Are you driving your passengers crazy with non-stop talking? You better not be on the cell phone, let alone texting.

To diagnosis a hypomanic episode, a feeling of euphoria lasting at least four days and three of the above symptoms must be present. If the mood is irritable, then four symptoms must be present. A manic episode is more severe than a hypomanic episode, usually with a decline in functioning. Hospitalization is often necessary to stabilize manic individuals and the warning light is always red.

Shall we tackle anxiety? That is a major undertaking as there are eleven different anxiety disorders. The most common diagnoses that I have seen in my practice are General Anxiety Disorder, Panic Disorder with or without Agoraphobia, Social Anxiety, Obsessive Compulsive Disorder – OCD, and Post-Traumatic Stress Disorder – PTSD.

You may not need a yellow light for me to diagnose General Anxiety Disorder. All I have to do is evaluate your driving posture. Your hands may be clutching the steering wheel so tight that your knuckles are white. Or is your seat on top of the steering wheel, your head jutting forward towards the windshield, and your foot barely touching the gas. If you look like that in your car, I guarantee I will pass you, because you are a menace on the road. You need to get a grip, and I am not referring to the one on your steering wheel. Pop some relaxation tapes in, please. You see, you have excessive worries, and one of them is most likely being in an MVA. Well, I guarantee you will have a motor vehicle accident if you don't manage your anxiety better. Medicine and/or therapy can help.

Panic Disorder results when panic attacks become so debilitating that people avoid leaving the home. Many of my patients get heart palpitations, become nauseous, get sweaty, feel a sense of doom and gloom, and actually either pull over to the side of the road or go to the nearest ER to rule out a heart attack. Again, this condition can be managed.

Ever drive with someone with OCD? Their dashboard is very sensitized to dust and clutter. The yellow light shines despite the shiny car. Actually OCD is a serious condition that has a wide spectrum ranging from cleanliness symptoms or traits, to a severe debilitating disorder. Serotonin agents have shown efficacy in treatment.

PTSD results from a near death experience and the onset of three clusters of symptoms. I worked at the VA and saw my fair share of Vietnam Vets burdened with this condition. Individuals who have also been in car accidents can have re-experiencing symptoms and flashbacks just by getting into the car. The whole dashboard would light up, and unless they are in treatment, would have to jump out to prevent further anxiety. Avoidance symptoms can actually result in some clients refusing to drive again. And heightened body arousal symptoms can lead to anger management problems and sleep insomnia.

So the dashboard can be a tool in alerting you to some warning signs of emerging symptoms. If you are willing to recognize that there might be a problem and are therefore willing to follow-up with someone you trust, then we have taken the first step to improving your mental health and wellness. We can develop a diagnosis and a treatment plan.

Part Three

The Journey
or
"The Many Roads We Have Traveled"

Chapter 18

Off-road Journeys
or
"My Favorite Ice Cream Flavor is Rocky Road"

We have, up until this point, been focusing on the biological or genetic aspects of our makeup in Part 1 and the psychological aspects that comprise our coping mechanisms, define our personalities, and make us the drivers we are today, in Part 2. But all through the text, we have referred to some of the stressors that together, with our genetics and psychological makeup, make up our GPS system. It's like a discussion of which came first, the chicken or the egg? Just because Part 1 and Part 2 were separate entities, the dynamics involved in coping with stressors had to be initiated from the very beginning. The intensity of the journey directly influenced our ability to drive. The journey may have triggered biological influences to be manifested. So as we explore the journey, we can only do so with the car and driver in place.

Can you remember your first journey? My early memories contain some very fortunate ones, because they were filled with love and support. I remember being in a green and white Buick four-door sedan stuffed with family and wonderful times. Christmas memories were the best. Holidays were filled with love, with giving, with lots of good food, and Charlotte's Belgium waffles.

I always ask my clients to discuss their holiday plans. Their past journeys influenced their current motivation to either embrace it or pray for its fast passage.

Childhood memories are critical in mapping our way. We

either leap into the car like my dog when I mention "car ride" (well he insists on my lifting his back legs, but the front paws are very enthusiastic), or we may prefer to leave the keys dangling on the wall indefinitely.

In addition to memories from our past causing some stress that put our driving skills to task, the social stressors that we are exposed to on a day-to-day basis will certainly affect the pleasantries of the journey.

I have seen young adults who navigated high school well. But the pressures of college, whether academic in nature or involving peer pressure or loneliness (I was so homesick at Thiel my freshman year), can cause onset of depression, substance abuse, or even schizophrenia. As I mentioned before, the journey can cause some familial tendencies to emerge.

Being raised in a small, steel town outside of Pittsburgh, I was very fortunate to have a loving and supportive family as I mentioned earlier. I had no idea that we were lower middle class based on my dad's income at the factory. My home life was wonderful, and there were always meals on the table. We lived above my Pup-Pup and Aunt Betty in a wonderful home on Second Avenue. Pup-Pup owned a small Clover Farm grocery store in our very own backyard. Every time I entered that garage-sized space, I would stick my nose in the coffee grinder to smell the wonderful aroma. God bless him – he wanted me to have that very coffee grinder when he died. Tuesday was the worst day of the week, because it was "liver for dinner night," followed by piano lessons with my sister, Eloise. That was my extent of misery at home.

However, behind my home ran an alley where all of the children in the block gathered to play. Hopscotch was my favorite. My needle on my self-esteem meter dipped as I left our second floor home and joined the other children. I learned in the alley that I was "not as good" as they were. Because my religion did not believe in a purgatory, I was going directly to you know where. I was often excluded from games or named last on a team.

When I went on to high school, I was introduced to the notion that unless you belonged to the A-list, you were less important. I thrived academically and had some wonderful girlfriends. I think we were thought of as nerds. I played the piano for the high school choir, which brought me joy. But I was never popular. And popularity gave you status. I did not have a boyfriend, and I think I was the only known virgin in my senior year in college – yes college, folks.

Why am I discussing such intimate details? Because they paved my road. I noticed that journeys initially made to social events caused me to feel uncomfortable and inferior. I was back in that alley or in the halls of Tarentum High School.

I could go on and on about the bumps in my road. They made me cry, cringe, and even consider ending it at one point. But somehow, through awareness of my deficiencies in coping and that perceptions of myself were in error, I was slowly able to tolerate the slings and arrows of outrageous misfortune. I began to appreciate who I am. And who I am is all of my past experiences. I now embrace those hardships. Without them, I could not have been challenged. I could not have become the driver that I am now. I can navigate that bumpy road.

What journeys do you fear? Is your enjoyment of life kept at an arm's distance because you prefer to drive on smooth pavement? It's almost as if you have created orange barrels in your mind, indicating work ahead. You take the detour to avoid the inconvenience.

Well, I urge you all to exam those potholes and those bumps. What stressors are you incapable of handling, or at least compromise your driving skills? Have you ever considered getting out a shovel and some asphalt or whatever that smelly black tar concoction is and begin to repair the road?

I want you to enjoy life's journey. But you have to be willing to go along for the ride. Despite the past, despite the stressors, despite the driver you are, despite your family history, despite your biological flaws, you can change. You may see the road sign, "Past the point of no return" on the road, but that does not exist in our vocabulary. It should not exist in your mind.

I am so blessed to have become aware of how beautiful life can be. I am able to roll with the punches. No, it was not an overnight insight like Scrooge experienced. It took time. And I am willing, as so many other mental health professionals are, to take the time with you.

Chapter 19

The Unplanned Journey

Sometimes we can be asked to take a trip that was never planned. You weren't prepared for it. The trunk is void of any suitcase containing coping mechanisms that would assist you in this particular journey. Nor did you ever contemplate, in your whole life, that this was part of your itinerary.

On Sunday, January 11, 2004, I came down to the kitchen to the smell of my husband's pancakes. "Where's Andy?" I asked Jim. He would never stay at a friend's home overnight without a phone call. I immediately called him and got his voice mail. I left a scolding but a concerned message at 9 A.M. Fifteen minutes later he called and apologized for not calling. His former college roommate was in town, and he fell asleep on the couch. He promised to be home soon, and he was. And he looked none the worse for wear, and unfortunately I suspected nothing.

So on Friday morning, January 16, I walked out the door at 8 A.M. on my way to work and noticed that his car was not there. Should I call him again, or should I scold him when he gets home? After all, his college roommate was home. I left for work, planning to call him around noon. At 11 A.M. I received a call from my husband. He said that I was to immediately go to the hospital ER. Andy was there. He had no other information at the time.

God bless my husband. He knew Andy's fate as soon as he entered the ER parking lot. He was met by the social worker who asked when I would be joining him. The social worker refused to say anything more until I arrived. Well, they didn't know my husband. He was thinking of me and wanted to know the news first. He would not have me hear the worst words ever spoken in a small "family room" in an ER by a stranger. He met me in the parking lot to give me the heart-breaking news. Andy had died. He had experimented with heroin with his friend. He snorted it and got very ill, lying on the bathroom floor of his friend's all night. His friend called the drug dealer who assured him that "kids get sick when they try heroin." The next time the friend checked on my dear son, he was not breathing and 911 was finally called. He was pronounced dead at the ER. My beautiful nineteen-year-old son whose smile could light up a room lay on a gurney with breathing tube in place. He still looked so handsome with his brown hair somehow perfectly parted in the middle. He was surrounded by two police officers that chastised me as I approached him, stating that I was not to touch him – "He's a coroner's case." I asked permission to touch him over the sheet, promising not to disturb the so-called crime scene.

I have multiple regrets from that day. First of all, I will always regret not calling Andy that morning. It was 8 A.M. Could he have answered the phone, or would his friend have had the courage to let me know what was going on? I will never know, but the doubt led to an incredible amount of guilt on my part.

Secondly, I wish I had kicked the policeman in the balls that treated me like a criminal and not a grieving mother.

Thirdly, I wish I had taken Andy into my arms and held him and whispered to him that I loved him and that he was now in God's care. Somehow, I think Andy knew this.

I debated whether to share the most devastating journey I have yet to encounter. But I also wanted to reassure you that I am OK. I am a survivor. I made lemonade. Andy's foundation was formed to help fight drug and alcohol use among teens and young adults. I no longer drink alcohol, not only as a tribute to my son, but also because of my family history. My dear friend, Joanna Connors, a wonderful journalist for the Cleveland Plain Dealer, devoted a series of articles regarding Andy's death, informing others that heroin was in the suburbs, not just in the inner city, and that it was a real problem. She documented our attempts to hold drug dealers accountable for selling drugs that resulted in a death. Surprisingly, we have been unable to get enough interest in enforcing a law to put those drug dealers behind bars, but I will continue to fight for that.

As a psychiatrist, I have had to restrain myself from jumping over my desk and shaking the shoulder of a client still grieving over the loss of his grandmother who died at age ninety-three some five years ago. Shame on me. Everyone has his or her own set of coping skills. Sometimes you can navigate that road as smoothly as possible, and other times a small bump can turn into an off road driving experience. It's like we just flooded the engine, and the car just won't start. We have to wait, count to ten, and gently put our foot on the gas to restart the engine.

Life is like that isn't it? Sometimes we have no idea how strong or weak we are unless we encounter a road hazard. Mother Theresa once said, "God will never give us more than we can handle. I wish he didn't have that much faith in me."

I know that I am a survivor. It was a lousy way of learning it, wasn't it? But we all have the capability of overcoming tragedy. I know this to be true. I need for you to believe that this is true, as well.

Chapter 20

Start your Engines!

Well, now that we are close to completing our little trip, I ask you these questions.

How would you describe your driving skills? I hope this book has enlightened you on that. What journeys do you plan to conquer? If you have not begun to examine these questions more closely after reading this book, then I am requesting that you pull your car to the side of the road and think this through. Put down that cell phone. I am not going to ask you that again.

If for any reason you find that your ability to complete today's journey is complicated by thoughts of previous journeys or that there are too many orange barrels on the road today, we need to talk.

I have offered to you a GPS system to better know yourself. I can help you steady the course. My goal is to have you enjoy the journey of life.

Impossible you say? Well, don't we have a little glitch in our git-along! Do we have to look under that hood again? Do we have to adjust your rearview mirror? Don't make me come over there and open up your glove compartment and see a neglected maintenance schedule.

We are in this journey together. Mental wellness is a reality, my dear friends. And I am here to offer it to you. Think of me as your driving instructor. I am a driving instructor who believes in you and in your ability to navigate life's challenging roads. And, of course, I wish for you the best of driving skills and good mental health.

I leave you with this Irish saying:

May the road rise to meet you.
May the wind be always at your back.
May the sun shine warm upon your face.
And rains fall soft upon your fields.
And until we meet again,
May God hold you in the hollow of His hand.

Good travels, my friends.

Appendix

To maintain mental wellness, we need a more concise guide to evaluate just how we are operating and managing our journeys.

I am providing you with a simple guideline in mnemonic form to help you conduct a systems survey of you. It is entitled "My Maintenance." Although it is self- explanatory, I will elaborate on how to interpret its use.

Now you will be able to reach into your own glove compartment and utilize a tool that will help you become more cognizant of just how you are doing. Please review your maintenance schedule at least every three months. An easier way to remember this is to do a seasonal check. After all, many individuals note some changes when the sun sets a little earlier, despite its bright orange hue. And don't we change the batteries in our smoke alarms twice yearly?

Although it is recommended to be reviewed every three months, sudden changes in any entry should be brought to the attention of your physician or psychiatrist.

In addition to "My Maintenance," I am including a "Mood Checklist" to enable you to gage just how you are feeling.

Every manual has a Troubleshooting section. However, since I am promoting mental wellness, this entire book has been devoted to "Troublepreventing". (Sorry to my spell checker but evidently that word doesn't exist either.) I am hoping to assist you in preventing any warning lights from developing. And should a yellow light appear, a problem is present. Just as you call your mechanic to discuss a problem, so must you pick up that phone and dial your physician or your psychiatrist to discuss any changes you have noted in your maintenance schedule.

My Maintenance

M – Medical health changes
Y – You (Be Kind to YOU!)

M – Mood
A – Appetite
I – Interests
N – Nighttime
T – Tension
E – Energy
N – New Changes
A – Attention
N – No Changes
C – Concentration
E – ETOH/drug Use

Using MY MAINTENANCE

Medical Health Changes – How is your medical condition? To expect your motor to run smoothly you need to maintain your physical health, as well. When was your last medical checkup? Are you aware of the preventative checklist that your medical doctor keeps in your chart? You better and you better be up-to-date. This is just a friendly reminder to check your calendar to note the last time you visited your primary care physician.

You – Are you taking care of yourself? Remember the stewardess' instructions on placing your O2 mask first? Well, are you taking the time to smell the roses? If you have not treated yourself to a bubble bath or some quiet time today, then please do so. You are so important. Take that buffing cloth out and shine your chassis.

Mood – I have provided a Mood Checklist as a guide to identify your feelings. Any instability, depression, or rapid swings in your mood should be reported to your physician.

Appetite – How has your appetite been? Any changes in your weight? A five percent change in weight either up or down is considered significant and an indication that something is wrong either mentally or physically.

Interests – If you have never been a social butterfly, then so be it. But if you do note a decreased desire in your usual routine then please note this.

Nighttime – How is your sleep pattern? Are you contributing to poor sleep with excessive caffeine intake or filling the bladder too late at night? Are you perimenopausal? Are you constantly thinking about what needs to be done or focusing on a particular topic that plays like a broken record? If sleep problems persist, discuss this with your physician. Insomnia for some may be easily cured, or it may be a sign of a co-morbid condition such as depression.

Tension – Are you experiencing any tension or anxiety? Is this new since your last three month checkup, or are you usually a high octane person? Does your anxiety interfere with the way you interact with others? Have you experienced social anxiety? Do you note any obsessive-compulsive type of activity? Do you have any phobias? Do you experience panic attacks? How severe are they? Have you visited the emergency room, thinking you were having a heart attack but given a sedative and sent home? Make sure you discuss any changes with your physician.

Energy – Are you operating on all cylinders, or are you noting that you sputter and spurt? There are so many physical and mental conditions that can cause energy changes. Anemia and thyroid problems are just two examples of how medical conditions can affect energy levels. Decreased or increased energy can also be indicators of a mood disorder. Any significant changes obviously need to be reported to your physician.

New Changes – This very important topic on your checklist deals with any social changes and stressors that may present themselves. Divorce, job loss, caring for older parents, trauma, and death of a loved one are all examples of unplanned changes. How are you coping? At the next 3 month checkup, have the feelings and coping mechanisms associated with the event improved or worsened? Adjustment disorders, pathological grief, and PTSD are often associated with unexpected changes that can overwhelm our coping capacities. Professional help is needed.

Attention – Some individuals have difficulty with paying attention to details. I admit I often misplace my car keys. However, any significant change in your attention span should be noted and monitored. If this change causes a decrease in your ability to function, and you have not added any new over-the-counter medication or tried any newfangled diet or energy pills advertised on TV, then report this to your physician.

No Changes – This could be good. That is, if you were satisfied with how you were functioning before. However, do not be fooled. If you have been in a "funk" and cannot explain it, and it persists without change, then that is a significant thing to bring up with your physician, don't you think?

Concentration – Just as attention changes can be of concern to us, so can our concentration. Are you able to focus? Can you read a book or follow a TV program without any problems? It is always important to track our ability to concentrate as we continue to manage our daily affairs.

ETOH/Drugs – Let's be very honest about this behavior. Have you conducted the CAGE questionnaire on yourself? Have you noticed that you are self-medicating to cope or "get by"? Have family members commented on your substance use? No one can really help you unless you want help. And I hate the fact that most people need to "reach the bottom" before they begin to seek help. I will always ask you about this behavior and challenge you. Every physician should ask you about this behavior!

Mood Checklist

Ashamed – Feel very badly that you did not yield right of way.

Guilty – See ashamed. Go home and hide in garage.

Anxious – Pull seat up too far. Clench steering wheel.

Lonely – Wish someone were sitting on passenger side.

Shy – May wish someone were sitting next to you but relieved that you don't have to hear their commentary on your driving.

Frightened – Unable to leave garage.

Frustrated – You are in a hurry and hit every red light.

Irritable – On your way to road rage. Trigger middle finger getting itchy.

Angry – You know where I'm going. Road rage has been reached.

Bored – Daydreaming. Oops, just missed turn-off.

Confused – Not only missed turn-off but forgot where you were headed.

Cautious – Anticipates "stale green" light and stops before it turns yellow.

Confident – A superb driver. Insurance carrier now offering to pay your premiums.

Exhausted – Too many errands to run and running on fumes.

Overwhelmed – See exhausted. Don't even have the energy or strength to fuel up.

Jealous – You want that fancy car that just pulled up next to you.

Sad –You reach the end of the driveway and make the turn despite feeling blue.

Depressed – You reach the end of the driveway and can't make the turn.

Suspicious – Feel that the driver ahead of you is purposely driving slowly to annoy you.

Surprised – You are driving over the speed limit and see hidden cop car.

Shocked – You see red and blue lights blinking behind you.

Hysterical – You cry at the drop of a bird poop on your windshield.

Happy – A good feeling. You feel like heading to shopping mall but are in control of your budget.

Ecstatic – Oops. Hit shopping mall and decided that you needed to cash in college fund for that adorable fur coat.

Mischievous – Causing road rage in others and not caring.

Hopeful – You turn out of driveway, anticipating a wonderful day.

Acknowledgements

Obviously, this book would not have been possible without the many people and events in my life that have made me who I am today.

To my husband, Jim, and to Peter and Molly, I love you dearly. And extra kudos to my son-in-law, Jeremy Duchon, who never once made me feel stupid when I asked him over and over again about computer related things.

I especially want to thank my wonderful sisters, Eloise, Elyse, and Ellen, for the most precious memories that we shared from childhood and to the current ones we continue to magically make. I miss you, Mom and Dad. I think you would be proud of your whole family and how we have managed to turn out.

To my dear friends, too numerous to mention, who supported me in tough times and toasted me in good ones. Good curling to you all.

To Jerry Buckley, whose support and exceptional mantra helped strengthen me and made me a much better driver.

To the Cleveland Clinic, whose dedication to wellness removed all unhealthy vending machines and replaced them with healthy alternatives.

To John Negus, my honest-to-goodness car mechanic. Thank you for keeping me safe on the road.

And finally, to Dr. Lu-Jean Feng, Linda Haas, and Dr. Gaylee MacCracken, whose philosophy of physical and mental wellness was the inspiration for this book.

**BUSINESS
BOOKS**

The study of the mind: interactions, behaviours, functions.
Developing and learning our understanding of self.
Psyche Books cover all aspects of psychology and matters
relating to the head.